From Tibet to Egypt: Early Travels After a Late Start

by

Jeremiah A. Gilbert

Cyberwit.net
HIG 45 Kaushambi Kunj, Kalindipuram
Allahabad - 211011 (U.P.) India
http://www.cyberwit.net
Tel: +(91) 9415091004
E-mail: info@cyberwit.net

Printed at VCORE.

I will not follow where the path may lead,

but I will go where there is no path,

and I will leave a trail.

—Muriel Strode

Introduction

I started keeping a journal in my freshman year of high school. For about a month, my English class was joined by a student teacher, and she liked to have us begin each session by journal writing for five minutes. This allowed for about a page per entry in my letter size notebook. Over the years, I have kept up the practice of journaling and find I still like to write one page per entry, regardless of the size of the journal.

The travel tales in my prior collection, *Can't Get Here from There*, originated as content for my current website. This is why they are short—to allow for minimal scrolling online. Because of their brevity, I focused on individual incidents. What follows here is a little different. Before my current website, I had a site that focused on overall trips rather than specific events. For this site, I used journal entries that were written while traveling or soon upon my return. The site was originally created to share my Tibetan travels in 2006. As I traveled more, I added to the site. This site ended with Japan in 2014 when I realized I wanted to design a new site that focused more on photography.

On the old site, journal entries were presented not with dates but with titles, one entry per page, and I have maintained that approach here. Dates given for trips are the month they originated, though some went into the following month. Because of the way I designed the site, some entries covered more than one day, and some split a day into more than one entry. I omitted days when nothing really happened, assuming I even wrote a journal entry on those days. I tend to have an impressionistic quality to my journal writing, though I am always attracted to facts and figures I find interesting.

The journal entries collected here cover 2006, when I first began traveling, and end in 2010, the year my mother died, and I became engaged. This was also the time period I spent with my first travel camera, having switched from film to digital before heading off to Tibet. The travels described here were often with groups. I have never been opposed to joining tour groups, though I have found I prefer smaller groups to larger ones. Some people I have met on these travels have become lifelong friends I try to look up when I'm on the road (and they always have a room waiting for them when they come out my way).

The information recorded here was accurate as of the time it was noted. The world changes continually, so some information is now out of date. For instance, the statue of Lenin I visited in his hometown of Gori, Georgia was removed two weeks after my visit. Also, the construction of the expansion of the Panama Canal I witness in 2009 has now long been operational. I'm hoping to see it in action on a planned return visit.

J.A.G.

CONTENTS

JUL. 2006 – TIBET 13
SETTING OFF 14
REDEYE PROPHET 15
GOLDEN SUBTITLES 16
BIRTHDAY IN BEIJING 17
INTO TIBET 18
CHANTING & BARTERING 19
CARPETS & LAMAS 20
UNDER CONSTRUCTION 21
A CLEAR VIEW 22
BASE CAMP 23
DUSTY DECLINE 24
A LITTLE LESS BROWN 25
GHOST IN THE MONASTERY 26
A QUICK RECOVERY 27
LAST NIGHT IN TIBET 28
BACK IN BEIJING 29
BURNING BAD KARMA 30
FLYING SOLO 31
JUN. 2007 – MEXICO 33
AN UPGRADED START 34
A DAY OF DRIVING 35
THE ETHEREAL EXPRESS 36
EN ROUTE TO EL FUERTE 37
BIRTHPLACE OF ZORRO 38
BALLET FOLKLORICO 39
EIGHT THOUSAND FOOT QUEST 40
BARRANCAS DEL COBRE 41
THE ROAD TO CHIHUAHUA 42
THE RETURN 43
DEC. 2007 – PERU 45
OVERNIGHT TO LIMA 46

INTO THE WILD 47
MONKEYS, BIRDS, AND CAIMEN 48
CUSCO BOUND 49
CHRISTMAS IN CUSCO 50
A FREE DAY IN RUINS 52
THE ROAD TO OLLANTAYTAMBO 53
IMAGINED REMAINS 54
RECENTLY UNCOVERED RUINS 55
CUSCO REDUX 56
FLOATING ISLANDS 57
BACK TO LIMA 58
CLOSING THOUGHTS 59
JUL. 2008 – GUATEMALA AND HONDURAS 61
GUNS AND BUDDHAS 62
TEXTILES, MASKS, AND STATUES 63
CREATED BY FIRE 64
THE ROAD LESS TRAVELLED 65
THE TWO COPANS 66
SINGLE-HANDED PHOTOS 67
ANOTHER ROAD TO RUINS 68
MONOLITHS AND MOSQUITOS 69
IN THE DETAILS 70
GOING AND COMING 71
AUG. 2008 – COSTA RICA 73
WORK AND RAIN 74
MBA, ANYONE? 75
LEYDI AND THE TRAMP 76
COFFEE, SULFUR, AND LOTS OF WATER 77
JUN. 2009 – SPAIN, PORTUGAL, AND MOROCCO 79
INTO THE LABYRINTH 80
BULLS AND RAIN 81
THE WRITING ON THE WALL 82
MORE VIRGINS THAN ONE CAN COUNT 83
TOWERS, BEACHES, AND MOUNTAINS 84
DONS JUAN AND GIOVANNI WALK INTO A BAR 85
SOUTH TO NORTH 86

ANOTHER LABYRINTH 87
INTO THE RED CITY 88
HAREMS AND CAMELS 89
THE START OF SOMETHING BEAUTIFUL 90
NORTH TO SOUTH 91
THE RED FORTRESS 92
JUL. 2009 – CENTRAL EUROPE 93
THE GOLDEN APPLE 94
ENTERING BOHEMIA 95
WHAT HANGOVER? 96
JOSEF K. WAS HERE 97
THE LOVELY PIANIST 98
DEM BONES 99
TEPLICE NAD METUJI 100
REMEMBRANCE 101
A PLEASANT SURPRISE 102
WORKERS' PARADISE 103
UNEVEN SURFACES 104
OLD AND NEW 105
WHO NEEDS SLEEP? 106
DEC. 2009 – TUNISIA 107
LOST IN TRANSIT (DAY ONE) 108
LOST IN TRANSIT (DAY TWO) 109
TRAVELING LIGHT 110
EL JEM (A.K.A. THYSDRUS) 111
DIGGING IN THE DIRT 112
LOVE AND SALT 113
ENGLISH MAP, ARABIC SIGNS 114
BLAST FROM THE PAST 115
A CHRISTMAS MIRACLE 116
SCENTS AND SACRIFICES 117
CITY BY THE SEA 118
THE ADVENTURE CONTINUES 119
MAR. 2010 – PANAMA 121
THE PERSON YOU SEE WHEN YOU'RE YOUNG 122
THE FOUR PIRATES 123

MIGHTY BIG LOCKS 124
HALF A CANAL 125
WHAT WOULD CRISTOBEL THINK? 126
TATTOOS AND DANCING INDIANS 127
SAINTS AND CHICKEN WIRE 128
AND THE LIST GOES ON AND ON 129
OLD TOWN PANAMA 130
LESSONS LEARNED 131
MAY 2010 – SOUTHERN CAUCASUS 133
HIGH ON A PLANE 134
RUSSIANS AND CHRISTIANS 135
BOOKS, GENOCIDE, AND DRIED FRUIT 136
TWO DAYS IN RUINS 137
A DAY OF MONASTERIES 138
INTO GEORGIA 139
OLD THEN NEW 140
GOLDEN FLEECE (AND LEMONADE) 141
THE BAD SEA 142
SACRIFICIAL LAMBS 143
CAVES, DESTRUCTION, AND SORE LEGS 144
NATIVE SON 145
MY ACHING LEGS 146
GOODBYE, GEORGIA 147
NO COUNTRY FOR TALL MEN 148
BAKU BOUND 149
CAESAR GERMANICUS WAS HERE 150
JUN. 2010 – WESTERN BALKANS 151
DOMESTIC IN DUBROVNIK 152
THE BLACK MOUNTAINS 153
AN INADVERTENT WINK 154
LONG DRIVE TO A SMALL ISLAND 155
BOSNIA TIMES THREE 156
SLIGHT CHANGE OF PLANS 157
SMALL TOWN SARAJEVO 158
TWO NIGHTS IN SPLIT 159
RUINS FOR A CHANGE 160

JUL. 2010 – LONDON, VENICE, AND BRUSSELS 161
AN AMERICAN TOURIST IN LONDON 162
CAMERA CONFUSION 163
BRIGHTON IN PRINT AND ON FILM 164
USE YOUR IMAGINATION 165
VENETIAN WEEKEND: FRIDAY 166
VENETIAN WEEKEND: SATURDAY 167
VENETIAN WEEKEND: SUNDAY 168
ST. ALBANS AND VERULAMIUM 169
THE BRIDGES OF CAM 170
HAMPTON COURT GARDENS 171
BELGIUM GETAWAY: FRIDAY 172
BELGIUM GETAWAY: SATURDAY 173
BELGIUM GETAWAY: SUNDAY 174
SALISBURY AND STONEHENGE 175
OFF THE BEATEN PATH IN BATH 176
MIND THE GAP 177
DEC. 2010 – EGYPT 179
FROM SNOW TO DESERT 180
TOUCH, DON'T TOUCH 181
STAIRWAY TO HEAVEN 182
TWO EVENTFUL NIGHTS 183
KARNAK THE MAGNIFICENT 184
SLOW BOAT TO EDFU 185
JIGSAW TEMPLE 186
ABU SIMBEL 187
ANOTHER CAMEL 188
TEMPLES AND TOMBS 189
MORE TEMPLES AND TOMBS 190
OUT OF AFRICA 191
IN MEMORIUM 192
ALSO BY JEREMIAH A. GILBERT 193

Jul. 2006 – *Tibet*

A 34-year-old me set off for Tibet, having been out of the country only one time before: Vancouver Island, British Columbia. I read once that Canada could be thought of as a gateway country to foreign travel for Americans, which was certainly true in my case. Originally, the tour I wanted to take approached Tibet through Nepal but, due to unrest in that country, it was changed to originating in China. Beijing, to be specific. The new train from Beijing to Lhasa had opened a few days before our arrival. However, we took the more traditional approach of flying from Beijing to Lhasa through Chengdu. Being inexperienced, I overpacked, taking too many clothes and not nearly enough money. The author of what follows had published his first collection of poetry, In a Strange Land, *only two years prior. This is probably why he thought it was a good idea to attempt a daily "haiku" during this trip.*

SETTING OFF

I have always wanted to do more traveling but have never had the time or money. Now that I have both (sort of), I decided to jump in and go to Tibet. I have been studying Buddhism off and on for the past twelve years, so Tibet is a country familiar to me. I've also been in a transition phase for the past year and a half. Having ended a long-term relationship and moving from years of struggling as an adjunct instructor to now being a full-time professor, this seemed like the place I needed to be.

Tibet is the highest region on Earth, with an average elevation of 14,000 feet (4,380 meters). I've received the recommended vaccinations and have a bottle of Diamox in my daypack, which is used to treat altitude sickness. I've heard you cannot bring a picture of the Dalai Lama into Tibet, so I'm leaving my guidebook at home in case a Chinese official sees it and objects to something within it.

I spend the week before the trip getting everything ready and saying my farewells. I pack two large duffle bags for this trip, soon regretting their weight, size, and lack of wheels. I promise several people lots of photographs, and I plan on returning with as many as I can. This will be my first trip using a digital camera, but I have had it long enough to have gotten accustomed to it. I'm also planning to only shoot in color, which is something new for me.

All my goodbyes said

Now off into the unknown

Summer full of haze

REDEYE PROPHET

My day begins with a redeye flight from Los Angeles to New York. It's a five-and-a-half-hour flight followed by a four-hour layover until I meet my tour group before boarding the flight to Beijing. I foolishly hope I can get some sleep on the flight. Just before we leave, a middle-aged fellow sits beside me and we start to converse some. He's from Tanzania and is very interested in my upcoming travels. We talk for a while and all seems well, then it comes about: Have I found Jesus? The rest of the flight is his life story and how he discovered Jesus and how I need to also. So much for sleep.

The flight ends with this fellow saying he knows he will hear from me in a year when I invite him to my wedding. I don't have any prospects at the moment, but I tell him I'll see what I can do. We exchange cards as we arrive in New York. Now I kill four hours mostly in the food court at JFK. The flight for Beijing leaves at 4:30 pm and is thirteen hours long, making it the longest flight I've been on to date. My group is nowhere to be found, and I start to feel a little anxious as our guide has my passport and Chinese visa. He finally arrives and quick introductions are made before we all queue to board our plane. Again, I'm hoping for some sleep during the flight but am not counting on it at this point.

Traveling at night

Salvation on an airplane

Wedding bells far off

GOLDEN SUBTITLES

The flight from JFK to Beijing flies over the Arctic, making for some breathtaking views from the window. I'm sitting beside one of my group and pass the time with idle conversation, cat naps, music, and finally by watching *The Chronicles of Narnia: The Lion, the Witch, and the Wardrobe*. For some reason, I'm enthralled with the idea of it being shown with golden Chinese subtitles. I also watch a Chinese film about a detective near retirement who is called into one last case. Good to know certain genre tropes are international.

Arrive in Beijing to the joys of baggage claim and customs, though both go relatively smoothly. On the way to our bus, a local offers to carry my bags and then demands the equivalent of $20 for the service. The city itself is crowded, everyone seems in a hurry, and the air is filled with pollution. When I mention the pollution to our local guide, she asks, "Don't you have bad air in Los Angeles?" "Yes," I counter, "but you can't chew it."

I'm looking forward to being off-line for the next few weeks—no cellphone or laptop on this trip. Our Beijing hotel is nice, though my roommate and I are put in a room with one bed while a couple on our tour has two twins in theirs, so we swap before having our first of many meals served with rice and eaten with chopsticks.

Once disconnected

The world continues to pass

With or without me

BIRTHDAY IN BEIJING

Today is my birthday. We begin our travels with a compressed city tour, including Tiananmen Square and the Forbidden City. It is hot and humid, which I come to realize is to be expected in Beijing in July.

Tiananmen Square contains the Monument to the People's Heroes, the Great Hall of the People, the National Museum of China, and the Mausoleum of Mao Zedong, who proclaimed the founding of the People's Republic of China in the square on October 1, 1949. It is vast and challenging to photograph. On the other hand, the Forbidden City is both a place of extensive history and visual splendor. It was constructed from 1406 to 1420 and was the former Chinese imperial palace and winter residence of the Emperor between 1420 and 1924. We only explore a fraction of its vastness as the whole area would take days to survey. The way from the exit to our bus is filled with beggars. One decides to grab onto my arm until I give her some money, which I do right before entering the bus so no one else will get the same idea.

Then we're off to explore a section of the Great Wall. I've dreamed of seeing the Great Wall since learning about it in grade school. Like the pyramids of Egypt, it is something that captures the imagination for life, and I never imagined standing on it on my birthday.

Birthday in Beijing

Far from the usual one

Of delis and books

INTO TIBET

We leave Beijing to catch a flight for Lhasa, the largest city in Tibet. The flight has a layover in Chengdu. While we are on the same flight and in the same seats for both legs of the flight, we have to exit the plane with all of our belongings in Chengdu. We will be doing this again on our return to Beijing, I'm told. Fortunately, I only have one carry-on. Unfortunately, like the roads in Beijing, getting on and off the plane is an everyone for themselves ordeal.

On the way to our hotel, we stop to view the Blue Buddha near Nethang Monastery, which is carved into the side of a mountain and surrounded by prayer flags—colorful rectangular pieces of cloth strung together to offer blessings to the surroundings. This is also our first opportunity to cross a street in Tibet. I'm beginning to develop a working theory that nothing has the right of way in China, except for maybe a yak.

Our hotel for the next few nights is near both the Barkhor (pilgrimage site and marketplace) and the Jokhang, the most revered religious structure in Tibet. Our hotel's street requires clearing a military checkpoint, the first of many that we will encounter while exploring Tibet. While China asserts that Tibet is not an occupied country, it certainly has the feel of one at times like these, when papers are being check by military officials.

Pilgrims, beggars, monks

All circle the marketplace

Among bartered deals

CHANTING & BARTERING

We begin our day with a visit to the Potala Palace. Founded by the Fifth Dalai Lama in the 17th century, it served as home to the Dalai Lamas until the current one's flight from Tibet during the Cultural Revolution. It is divided into a Red and a White Palace and is an architectural marvel. It is a steep climb up that most of us take slowly as we've yet to acclimatize to the altitude of Lhasa (around 12,000 feet or 3650 meters). Little, old Tibetans, on the other hand, hurry up the way as if they were at sea level.

Later we are given an hour to roam the Barkhor before attending a chanting session at the Jokhang. Unfortunately, I make a wrong turn in search of something cold to drink and end up down a very aggressive lane of the Barkhor. At one point, I have three vendors holding me in place while I barter over a singing bowl. After thirty minutes, I end up with two bowls and a bracelet for less than half of what the one bowl I was sort of interested in was initially priced at.

Sitting in the Jokhang listening to the monks chant is an incredible experience. Many of us find it quite meditative by the end and are sorry when it is over. The tour I have joined mainly consists of college students who can receive credit for their travels by attending some lectures along the way. While these lectures are optional for those of us not seeking credit, cultural experiences such as this one are to be experienced.

Yak butter candles

Scent the guttural chanting

Mind there and away

CARPETS & LAMAS

It is the current Dalai Lama's birthday. We start the day with a visit to a carpet factory run by a co-op of Tibetan families. As sales go directly to the families, many of us buy at least one rug, though some buy many more. While some buy enough to warrant shipping home, I purchase a small, square meditation carpet that I tuck into the end of one of my duffel bags. While waiting for the others to complete their transactions, I sit along the roadside and photograph my surroundings, including some passing cows, a monk in a cowboy hat, and the prayer wheel painted on the side of our tour bus.

Visit two monasteries during the day. First is Drepung Monastery, which was built in 1416. While there, we receive an audience with Lama Lobsang Tenzin Rinpoche, the current abbot of Drepung. Somehow, I get lost on my way to the meeting area and end up surprising some monks in an area I'm clearly not meant to be in. Apologizing through hand gestures, I backtrack, hitting my head along the way, and find my group. Later we visit Sera Monastery to watch the monks debate. Unfortunately, we are too late for the debate, but we do get to watch the monks chant. Before dinner, we stop by a thangka studio. Thangkas are a Tibetan Buddhist painting on fabric usually depicting a Buddhist deity, scene, or mandala. Here we are shown how select minerals are turned into paint, how the thangkas are painted, and are given a chance to purchase some.

In his simple room

The Lama speaks of healing

And true compassion

UNDER CONSTRUCTION

Leave Lhasa today headed for Shigatse, the second-largest city in Tibet. We switch from a tour bus to Land Cruisers as the road is under construction in many places, sometimes requiring off-roading to get around it. We're four to each vehicle. While I'm usually up front due to my height, one in my group suffers from motion sickness and needs to be upfront. This leaves me in the back, which is hard on the back and knees.

For our last night in Lhasa, we went to a restaurant that featured a musical show. I get a little creative using a longer shutter speed to try to capture some motion with the dancers. I also have to time my shots between the ones where the mainland Chinese in attendance stand in front of the stage to get themselves in photos being taken by someone else in their group. I'm beginning to realize that manners are a hindrance in China.

In the morning, we stop by an orphanage. We are given a tour, and some of us leave donations. Many of the coeds in our group want to take a Tibetan child home with them. Later we stop to see where some incense is being made. In Shigatse, we have Tibetan-style rooms, which prove to be the most comfortable so far. I was warned before this trip how hard Tibetan beds can be, but I've quite enjoyed them so far and will consider getting a firmer mattress upon my return home. Our last bit of luxury before heading to Everest.

The end of pavement

Real adventure now begins

Lungs filling with dust

A CLEAR VIEW

Day of traveling heading for Tingri, often used as a base by mountain climbers preparing to ascend Mount Everest. It is also known for its views of Mount Everest, Mount Lhotse, Mount Makalu, and Cho Oyu—four of the six highest mountains in the world. We begin the day at Zhashenlunbu Temple, founded by the first Dalai Lama in 1447. I have not photographed much within temples and monasteries primarily out of respect, but I did have to photograph the Maitreya Buddha Statue here. It cost me ¥75 (about $10) but is well worth it. Here we also get to witness the monks debating, which is an remarkable experience. As an admirer of Zen, I have never seen anything quite like it.

We make many stops along the way, and I take some photos at each, avoiding the side of the road others are using as a pit stop. At one pass, we reach our highest elevation of the trip at 17,100 feet (about 5,200 meters) and also catch our first glimpse of Everest, or Chomolungma ("Goddess Mother of the World") in Tibetan. It is a wonderfully clear view, which our guide tells us is rare. Having read Jon Krakauer's *Into Thin Air,* I do not have any desire to climb it but have to admire its beauty.

It's been a long day of travel, and I retire early to bed. We'll be at base camp in the early afternoon tomorrow.

Clear sky with few clouds

Seems like the Mother Goddess

Enjoys our esteem

BASE CAMP

Only a half-day of travel today. One of our pit stops overlooks a small village. As we stretch our legs, one can see a line of children head from the village toward our caravan of Land Cruisers. Fortunately, we each seem to have a little something to give them when they arrive. Just before we're ready to leave, one last little girl can be spotted heading our way. We scramble to find something between us to give her as she's red-faced and panting when she reaches us.

Just below Everest base camp is Rongphu Monastery. It was established in 1902, not making it very notable in terms of antiquity. Still, it does lay claim to being the highest monastery in the world at an elevation of around 16,400 feet (5000 meters). Here I photograph it and the surrounding area. I must admit to being repeatedly distracted by Everest.

We then drive up to base camp. There is a series of tents here, some with names like Hotel California. One is also a Post Office selling postcards to send home. After some time exploring, we are given the option to either drive back to Rongphu Monastery for a lecture or hike back. I choose to walk it. It takes two hours at an elevation between 17,000 and 16,400 feet, but the experience is invigorating. This region is believed to be an ancient riverbed, and some beautiful river rocks can be found along the way, one of which may have found its way into my daypack.

High elevation

Cold wind through leather and bones

Unforgettable

DUSTY DECLINE

Another long day of traveling. During the past few days, the dust has given me a permanent, minor sore throat, and I haven't showered in days as there has been no hot water when there has any water at all, relying on wet wipes for the body and a hat for the hair. Early into our departure, we stop to photograph some yak. I've photographed my fair share of yak already, so I just play observer for a change.

Most of the day is spent backtracking, so I have already photographed a lot of the terrain. We stop at the same overlook we did two days ago. When we were here previously, an old woman started draping me in white Tibetan ceremonial prayer scarves called kataks. She's back, and I'm covered in kataks again. Guess I know what souvenirs I'll be bringing back from this trip. We stop midday to have a picnic lunch in a field. It's basic sandwiches with chips and water, but much appreciated. Afterward, we gather up what has gone unused, and it is donated to the locals who have been watching us in fascination.

Spend the night in Sakya. The promise of a hot shower goes unfulfilled. I'd even settle for a lukewarm shower, but there is no hot water whatsoever. Guess it's one more day of wet wipes and a hat. There are some distinct structures on the hill behind the hotel I am hoping to photograph in the morning.

Day spent in reverse

The left now becomes the right

Sky blue as before

A LITTLE LESS BROWN

In the morning, after breakfast, I go up to the roof of our hotel and photograph some of the remnants on the hill behind us. I want to hike up to them, but there is no time for that. We then head over to the Sakya Monastery, built in 1268. Before the Cultural Revolution, it was one of the largest monasteries in Tibet. Its Mongolian architecture is quite distinct from that of temples we've visited. This is the second time on this trip I have meditated in a monastery, and it is a remarkable experience. There is such a silence present along with a sense of all the meditation that has occurred before.

While we make our way back to Shigatse, I take a few more photos in transit. I have never been anywhere with such a wonderful sky and find any excuse I can to photograph it. Prayer flags are also becoming a common photographic feature. They are everywhere you look in Tibet, providing a splash of color and good karma.

Finally, get a shower in Shigatse. The water coming out of my hair is decidedly brown, looking like chocolate milk as it heads from my hair to the shower floor. I hang out in the hotel's bar with some of my group before heading to dinner and then retire to another early night after another long day of travel.

Incense and candles

Silence engulfed in silence

Offerings abound

GHOST IN THE MONASTERY

Wake up in the middle of the night a little nauseous with heart palpitations. By the morning, there is full nausea, which is uncommon for me. Fortunately, it is a short travel day. We begin by visiting Tashilhunpo Monastery, where a vast tangka is on display, comprised of three 100 foot (30 meter) tall pieces. Our guide informs us that some of the monks here are believed to be secret police.

As the day progresses, I become more and more light-headed and am subject to bouts of not being able to catch my breath. We visit the Pelkor Chöde Monastery, but the air inside is too dense for me, filled with the scent of burning incense and candle wax, so I rest awhile in the courtyard. I snap a few photos to pass the time. I think one of the younger monks thinks I am a ghost because I have become so pale.

By lunch, I can hardly stand. Tenpa, our guide in Tibet, gets me to the hotel in Gyantse and supplies me with oxygen. I rest some. When I awake, I have an incredible fever. I take some medicine, but nothing seems to help. I fall back asleep. It is a restless night accompanied by a thunderstorm outside. Before heading off on this trip, I attended a weekly meditation practice and recall a visualization that we had been taught. So, I attempt to meditate in my delirious state, visualizing my fever as a fire burning within me, and slowly focus on putting it out.

Do not blame the sky

If it so happens to rain

That is its role then

A QUICK RECOVERY

In the morning, I wake up, and all of my ailments have gone. My roommate notes that I don't sound like I'm in pain anymore, which I take to be a good sign. Tenpa had been on the phone the night before with the hospital in Gyantse, who were ready to admit me if my fever didn't break. While I have no recollection of it, apparently he had been coming to check on me every few hours, applying a cold washcloth to my forehead.

We begin the day with a visit to the Rabse Nunnery. It is noticeably cleaner than the monasteries we have visited. We have a brief tour and then meditate in their small hall. The nunnery was moved to its current location in 1985 after two original monasteries further up in the hills were destroyed during the Cultural Revolution. A maze of streets from the nunnery leads to the old town along a path that follows the hillside's contours and offers arresting views of a fort in the distance.

More photos snapped in transit to Tsedang. We take a slight detour up a winding mountain road to view Yamdrok Lake, a sacred lake in Tibet that runs a deep shade of turquoise. Having lived for a few years in the mountains, I'm okay with the winding conditions up to the lake. However, the others in my Land Cruiser are not and repeatedly ask the driver to slow down. Where's the fun in that?

Day ends with water

One of the four holy lakes

Sublime before us

LAST NIGHT IN TIBET

Sometimes you have to break the law in order to get a good photo. Fortunately, another in my group agrees, so we both cross over a barbed-wire fence to remove power lines from a view of some dunes before setting off for the day.

Today is spent at Samye Monastery. To get there, it is about an hour's drive, followed by an hour's boat ride, followed by a half-hour of off-roading. Samye is Tibet's first monastery, dating back over 1200 years. If you climb the hill behind Samye, you discover that it is shaped like a mandala. I make it about three-fourths up the hill when it dawns on me that I was sick in bed only two days before, so I play it safe, take some photos from my elevated vantage point, then head back down. I start to head for the restroom upon my return to the monastery, but the smell leads me to believe it hasn't been cleaned since Samye was first built. Instead, I head to a shop to purchase a mystery juice I have been drinking my whole time in Tibet—I think it might be orange and carrot.

Our last night in Tibet. A group of us hangs out for a while at a nearby bar, though our guide has warned us not to mix alcohol and altitude. Some Chinese businessmen seem keen on buying drinks for the pretty Western coeds in our group, which is when a few call it a night. Those who stay end up breaking a table while dancing on it.

Everything must end

One of the hardest lessons

Lightning in the sky

BACK IN BEIJING

On our way to the Lhasa airport, we stop at Yumbulagang Palace, the oldest structure in Tibet. According to legend, it was the first building in Tibet and the palace of the first Tibetan king. It stands on a hill on the eastern bank of the Yarlung River, and one can either hike up to it or hire a horse (there's even a camel). From its heights, one can see India and trace the current Dalai Lama's escape route during the Cultural Revolution. While others explore these heights, I decide to explore the lower regions, taking some assorted photos of the settlement below the palace.

At our layover in Chengdu, we disembark with all our belongings as we did before, some now carrying considerably more than when we did this on our way to Tibet. We don't arrive in Beijing till late in the evening, though it is still hot and humid. Too late for dinner, most of us retire to our rooms, sorry to find our stay in Tibet over. The husband-and-wife company running this tour also offers another Tibet tour that several of us are now considering. The husband, who has been our overall guide for this trip, also informs me that now that I have survived Tibet, I am ready for India, another location his company offers tours to. He's also quite impressed that I started my travels with Tibet.

Back in the city

With its crowds and endless smog

Like being back home

BURNING BAD KARMA

A free day in Beijing. A group of us heads to the Summer Palace by way of the metro and a ferry. It is hot and humid, and a long walk to the metro, in what we think is the right direction. We're just about ready to quit when one of us spots the metro sign. Once there, it runs very smoothly and is surprisingly not crowded, though it is Sunday. To get the ferry we need to take, we were told to head in the direction of the building with what looks like a tall television antenna on it at our metro stop. However, there are five buildings with such towers, each in a different direction. After heading in the wrong direction and nearly walking onto the freeway, a kindly middle-aged man leads us in the right direction. The ferry ride from the lower depths of samsara begins. It is crowded and hot and, when we get splashed by a passing speedboat, somehow my face starts bleeding. When we think it's over, we discover that we have to board a second ferry that is even more crowded and has a Chinese woman with a megaphone.

When we finally reach the Summer Palace, we make it our mission to find the way out as quickly as possible as we're exhausted from getting there, and the megaphone is still ringing in our ears. Again, we have no idea if we're headed in the right direction but figure we just burned off enough bad karma in the ferries that we deserve a break. When we do find the exit, it's taxis to the Hard Rock Café, one of which isn't a taxi, but nobody cares at that point.

Too weary to write

One day in Tibet is worth

A thousand elsewhere

FLYING SOLO

Back from our exhausting Summer Palace excursion, I head to my room, trying to recover from the heat with a nap and a half gallon of orange juice I purchased in the lobby shop. Back among the living a few hours later, I run into a group of coeds from my group who ask what I'd been up to and, when I mentioned the Hard Rock Café, they got very excited. So, on my last night in Beijing, I return to the Hard Rock Café with its glorious air conditioning and familiar food.

Thirteen hours back to New York. This time it seems to pass a little more quickly. Someone spots that the most active from our group is holding an energy drink. Not wanting her to be running up and down the aisles all flight long, I offer to take it as I probably won't be sleeping anyway. No new films to watch, so I end up watching King Kong to pass the time, though I honestly have no interest in it. Why do they keep remaking it? Delay at baggage claim when no one's bags appear at first. Finally, bags start to arrive, and it's time for us to say our farewells. A mild panic brews as there are still two of us without luggage, but our bags eventually arrive, and it's one last goodbye and hug.

I then realize I'm back to being alone. I flew out on my own, but after spending the past few weeks with this group, I certainly notice that they are gone. It's dinner on my own before flying back to Los Angeles. Once home, I awake in the night uncertain of where I am, preferring where I had been.

Suddenly alone

The shortest flight of the day

Becomes the longest

Jun. 2007 – *Mexico*

It's been nearly a year since my Tibet trip. Being an inexperienced traveler, that trip cost me more than it should have, so I've needed to save up. Having thoroughly enjoyed my journey, my mind started wondering where I could head off to next. While I only live a two-hour drive from the Mexico border, I'm sorry to say I had never been. As the first town across the border is Tijuana, I bought into the concerns about safety I'd heard growing up. Now seeing it as a viable travel option (and more than just Tijuana), I start investigating options. There are 32 federal entities in Mexico—31 states and the capital, Mexico City, a separate entity without being formally a state, much like Washington, D.C. in the United States. Its history is rich and vast, and I soon find myself spoiled for choice. I opt for an experience for this first time on the train to Copper Canyon, though future trips will involve Mayan ruins and a shamanic sacrifice.

AN UPGRADED START

Barrancas del Cobre, or Copper Canyon, is a group of six distinct canyons in the Sierra Madre Occidental in the southwestern region of the state of Chihuahua in northwestern Mexico. The combined length of its ravines makes Copper Canyon four times larger than the Grand Canyon. In some places, it's even deeper, with a depth of over 1 mile (1.6 km). The walls of the canyon are a copper color, which is the origin of its name.

I have always heard that the train ride into Copper Canyon is one of the finest there is, so I have decided to give it a try this summer. The last time I was on a train was when my fifth-grade class took Amtrak down to the San Diego Zoo, and I fell in love with the observation car. Unfortunately, I did not fall in love with the bus ride from the train station to the zoo that demanded exact change and seemed to make stops every other block.

I was contemplating two tours for this trip, one originating in Tucson and one in El Paso. Figuring they both board the same train, I decide to go with the more affordable option. Upon my arrival at the hotel, I find that my room key does not work. When I tell the front desk, a manager escorts me back to the room to try the key for himself only to find there is already a couple in what is supposed to be my room. Apologizing, he upgrades me to a suite, which I don't complain about. Too bad it's only one night in El Paso with a very early departure. But I make the most of it, reading in the living area before stretching out in a considerably larger bed than the one I usually sleep in.

A DAY OF DRIVING

The first full day is one of driving. We depart El Paso very early in the morning to try to beat the crush at the border. At first, the officials don't seem to notice our bus, so our guide asks the driver to pull into another lane to get their attention. The trick works, and we're soon all off the bus and line up to press the button that determines if one's luggage is inspected—green it's not and red it is. In all, it takes about an hour to cross into Mexico.

After driving through Juarez, we switch from our American bus to a Mexican one, which is similar, though a little smaller. This is a large tour, and every seat is taken. I'm sat beside the only other single traveler on our trip. Lunch is in the outskirts of Chihuahua, which we will return to at the end of our journey. On our way to Creel, we make a stop in La Junta. The photographer in me is getting anxious as it's been nearly a day without any photos taken, so I get in a few, though where we stop is anything but picturesque.

My room in Creel is far more rustic than my suite the night before, but it's grand compared to some of the accommodations in Tibet. My new rule: If you can sit on the toilet, it's a good room. Our group is offered a complimentary margarita upon arrival. For some reason, those that don't want theirs decide to pass them on to me. I'll be sleeping well tonight. I follow this by watching a few episodes of *The Simpsons* in my room dubbed in Spanish.

After a good night's sleep, I discover that I've brought along the world's worst disposable razor. After five minutes of ripping and tearing, I decide that I'll wait and see if I can find a better one in El Fuerte.

THE ETHEREAL EXPRESS

In the morning, I explore the town. Creel was historically a logging town, although tourism has become the primary job source over the last few decades because it is near Copper Canyon as well as Basaseachic Falls, one of the highest waterfalls in Mexico. I snap a few photos along the main avenue. Elections are coming, so there are many banners of candidates throughout the town. As tends to happen, I become a little obsessed with the carvings in the pillars along the roadside and take several close-up shots.

Following the morning's exploration of Creel, we head to the train station to await our train through Copper Canyon, ending in El Fuerte. According to locals, the train we are waiting on is known as the Ethereal Express because "Only God knows when it will arrive." Anything within an hour of its stated arrival is considered on time. Before heading to the station, I snap a few shots of them packing our luggage on a truck in tall stacks without tying the suitcases down. This might be the last I see of my suitcase.

While waiting for the train, I snap a photo of a girl selling apples and chocolate bars. She is very self-assured and stands with an arched back while holding her wears on a disposable plate. Creel has also been our first sighting of the Tarahumara natives. They prefer not to be photographed and typically avoid eye contact. We will encounter them throughout our trip as they reside all about the canyons.

The 11:15 a.m. train arrives at 11:45 a.m., so it's on time.

EN ROUTE TO EL FUERTE

It is a long train ride to El Fuerte. The train passes through 86 tunnels and crosses 37 bridges. The longest tunnel, "El Descanso," is over a mile in length and is the last tunnel before reaching El Fuerte. It takes over two minutes to pass through it. Our guide tells us that he times it each trip as the times can vary depending upon the engineer's desire to set a new record. Between the train cars, there is an open area to take photos. Still, with so many tunnels, I could easily see myself being so engrossed in snapping a photo that I don't see the tunnel coming. There is the end to my journey. Instead, I snap a few photos from my not-so-clean window.

We do make a brief stop at Divisadero, which overlooks three of the canyons in the area. I take a few photos of some of the wears available for sale, along with some shots of the canyons. We are only given twelve minutes for this stop and are told that after a long whistle blow, the train will leave without us, so I keep a close eye on the time. I also notice the woman I've been seated next to on the bus is talking to locals and handing out small booklets. Only later do I discover she's trying to get them to accept Jesus as their personal savior.

Back on the train, I snap some more shots from my window as we continue through the canyons and toward El Fuerte. A few rows behind me, at the back of our train car, are two armed guards, both with automatic rifles. Every so often, they get up to go up the aisle and into other compartments before making their way back to the seats a while later. Growing up, I'd always heard about how unsafe Mexico was, along with the occasional story of a Spring Breaker disappearing in Tajuana, the closest city to where I live. I don't know if the armed guards make me feel safe or uncertain.

BIRTHPLACE OF ZORRO

In El Fuerte, we stay at the Posada del Hidalgo. Built in 1890 by a wealthy and influential mayor, it is a beautiful colonial mansion. At the time of its completion, it was the largest mansion in El Fuerte. It is a lovely space with pillared arches undulating around central courtyards filled with lush fauna and central fountains. The Casa Vieja section of the hotel is believed to have been the original site of Zorro's house. The complimentary margaritas here are much better than those in Creel. I also discover a liking for Dos Equis during some free time at the bar, which is also home to some amazingly colorful hummingbirds.

Essentially a coastal town, El Fuerte is hot and humid this time of year. For many centuries it served as the most important commercial center in northwestern Mexico due to its proximity to the silver mines in the canyons. I start the day by taking some photos inside the former mansion. During the short bus drive the previous night, I saw several sites I wanted to photograph the following day, but none of them seem to be catching my eye this morning.

We then take a river float trip looking for birds. Everyone is covered in insect repellent as mosquitoes are prevalent. I don't wear any as they have never shown any interest in me and continue not to. Seated along the rear of the boat, I attempt to photograph some of the birds while also maintaining my balance. Fortunately, there is a birder among my group, saving me from also trying to read the provided pamphlet to identify what I am seeing. He is very keen on spotting them and letting us all know what he's spotted. I tend to be of the green bird, yellow bird variety of spotter. Oh, look, there's another brown bird.

BALLET FOLKLORICO

Before dinner on our last night in El Fuerte, we are treated to a ballet folklorico. I attempt to take some photos, but the light is dim and the room is small, so I abandon my efforts and focus on enjoying the show. There are four women and four men who perform two different styles of dance. Near the end of the second dance, each female dancer takes the sombrero from their male partner and uses it to select a man from the audience to come dance with them. One of the dancers chooses me, not realizing my near-total lack of dancing ability. To my knowledge, thankfully, no photos exist of this.

It is an early morning to catch the return train, this time ending in Barrancas, just south of Creel and situated along the edge of the canyon. I don't take any photos on the return trip. However, I do watch the guards periodically pass through our car, with either a pistol on their side or an automatic rifle on their back. As with the train ride down, they sit in the back of the car and occasionally walk up and down the aisle.

We arrive at our destination in the early afternoon. We've boarded an old school bus for the short drive from the train station to our hotel. There is no legroom, and my knees drive into the metal frame of the seat in front of me. Making up for the uncomfortable ride is our hotel, the Posada Barrancas Mirador, which is situated on the canyon's rim, and the views are breathtaking. Once we get settled in and have our compulsory margarita, I decide it's time to stretch my legs and go for a hike.

EIGHT THOUSAND FOOT QUEST

From the exquisite view afforded from the hotel's balcony, I notice a circular structure off to the south, which becomes the focus of my hike. I'm not exactly sure how to get there, but a brief exploration behind the hotel finds what turns out to be the beginning of a trail. As I begin to head out, I realize that I am alone and have told no one where I am going. I am also traversing along the edge of the canyon at an elevation of around 8000 feet (2400 meters) and left my hiking boots at home, so I'm attempting it with sneakers.

The hike is going well till I come across a short ladder missing its bottom rung. But there is a rock in the rung's place, so it's no problem climbing it. I continue along the boulders and narrow path until I come across a broken bridge, the first few planks of which are missing. This poses more of a dilemma. Never being one to let obstacles get in my way, I jump and continue on. My goal now in sight, I come across my last obstacle: a pole with notches cut into it acting as a ladder up to the structure I'm aiming to reach. It again comes to mind that I am alone and have told no one where I have gone. One slip and I'm off the edge.

After reaching my destination, I explore the area some then notice ominous clouds dumping rain to the east. I head back down to the hotel only to discover that several from my group had been following my hike with their binoculars, guessing at each obstacle whether I'd attempt it or turn back. "I really thought that bridge was going to stop you," one tells me. "Never thought you'd jump it," another confides.

It's happy hour at the hotel bar, so I indulge with a few piña coladas before calling it an early night.

BARRANCAS DEL COBRE

As I'd hiked up the day before, this morning I decide to hike down. It's a late start, however. Along with safety concerns in Mexico, I'd also always heard about Montezuma's revenge, a form of traveler's diarrhea that occurs due to eating or drinking contaminated food or water. To add to this, in El Fuerte, our local guide cautioned us against street tacos only to get ill from them himself that evening. All of this culminated in me popping anti-diarrhea tablets at the first sign of a slightly off stomach this entire trip, and now I am painfully constipated.

The Tarahumara are a group of indigenous people living in the state of Chihuahua that are renowned for their long-distance running ability. Originally inhabitants of much of Chihuahua, they retreated to the high sierras and canyons such as the Copper Canyon on the arrival of Spanish colonizers in the 16th century. The area of the Sierra Madre Occidental that they now inhabit is often called the Sierra Tarahumara because of their presence. Last night, while watching the sunset from my room's balcony, I could see their campfires in the distance.

There is a trail leading to a Tarahumara village behind our hotel. Once there, I feel like a trespasser, so I decide to explore away from the village. Our guide had brought in two Tarahumara the night before as part of a discussion, a woman in her eighties and a girl of six. After being very timid at first, the girl kept going back to the last row of people, where it turns out they were stuffing her pockets full of dollar bills. She also started playing a game with the woman seated in front of me, which lit up her face.

THE ROAD TO CHIHUAHUA

After a morning of exploring, we begin the journey to Chihuahua. Before leaving, we head back to the outlook at Divisadero, as this will be our last look at the canyons. I take some photos along with a couple of shots of the natives. I have been reluctant to photograph them but know they come to this area to sell their wares and are more receptive to outsiders. I also notice the other single in our group is back to trying to convert the natives to Christianity.

On the way to Chihuahua, we make a few stops. At one, there is a mission that I cross the street to photograph. As with China and Tibet, I'm not sure that anyone or anything has the right of way when crossing streets here as no one seems to slow down for pedestrians, so I'm quick about it. I cross with a fellow who has been to Machu Picchu, where I've been seriously considering going to for Christmas. I ask him lots of questions and he assures me that I should go.

We have a mariachi band at dinner, our third of the trip if my total is correct. While they are quite good, I'm enchanted with the woman making guacamole at our table. She is beautiful and clearly skilled. I'm contemplating proposing marriage and moving down here before I come to my senses. It must be all the margaritas that have been consumed this trip.

It's our last meal together, and the group sitting with me apologizes for my being stuck beside a woman trying to convert the local population the entire trip. I don't mind. I've always been able to get along with almost anyone, even when politically or theologically on opposite ends of the spectrum. She is originally from Mexico and lets me in on some of the sights to see in her country, which I have been making mental notes of.

THE RETURN

We have a free day in Chihuahua. Wanting a day to explore and not think about photography, I leave my camera in my room as I head out with a duo from my group to try to locate the largest bookstore in town. They are a gay couple near me in Los Angeles. One of them is a pianist and just completed his second time as an entertainer on a world cruise. He's also a Vietnam vet and confesses that he couldn't bring himself to disembark in Vietnam on the first world cruise. This set an intention within him to disembark on the second cruise, and he found the whole experience cathartic.

They are looking for a specific title and figure this bookstore would have it. I'm just looking forward to the walk and some company in a new city. Of course, we only have the vaguest of directions and no specific address. After a few hours of circling the same area in the midday sun, we decide to give up and return to our hotel for a rest. In my room, I look up the bookstore in the directory provided and find that it was on a side street.

The following day is the drive to Juarez and the border crossing. Last time we had to take out all of our luggage and stand in line to push a button. If the light turns green, you're free to go; if the light turns red, you're not. This time it's another line, but this time with only our carry-ons and no buttons. As before, it takes about an hour and then it's off to the airport. I'm let off first as I have the earliest flight. As always, it's a cramped plane seat, and the person in front of me insists on reclining in their seat.

Good to know some things never change.

Dec. 2007 – *Peru*

I have always been attracted to ruins, whether they be of ancient civilizations or failed modern enterprises. In Southern California, most ruins are not very old and do not last very long, often toppled over to make room for the next failed endeavor. Many of these "ruins" I have photographed around where I live no longer exist. One place nearby was demolished six months after photographing it to make way for a church that never was constructed. Another was gone only two weeks after photographing it, the area replaced with mammoth, rectangular warehouses. This time the ruins I am pursuing are much older—the lost civilization of the Incas, Machu Picchu. While this is the main attraction of Peru, my trip was not just to see Machu Picchu. This trip begins with a flight to Lima, then a flight to Puerto Maldonado, our entryway into the Amazon. From there, another flight to Cusco, which then leads into the Sacred Valley, culminating with Machu Picchu. Finally, a drive to Puno, a port city along Lake Titicaca, the highest navigable lake in the world.

OVERNIGHT TO LIMA

I fly to Lima from Los Angeles via El Salvador. It's an overnight flight, though I do not expect to get much sleep. For some reason, I fly out in business class, though my return is economy. This is my first time in anything other than economy class. Along with a wide, comfortable seat and legroom, I'm surprised when the striking Costa Rican woman I noticed at the gate is seated beside me. She orders champagne to help her sleep and is incredibly friendly. We talk for a bit, and I begin to wonder why I'm not heading to Costa Rica. After a while, I do get some sleep and awaken with her resting her head on my arm. I'm now thinking I should fly business class from this moment on.

Quick layover at the San Salvador airport. A simple rectangular layout of an airport, with some nice shops lining its narrow halls. My Spanish is poor at best, so I'm not sure what's being said over the loudspeaker at the gate, though I assume the flight is boarding when everyone gets up and starts heading for the gate. I notice there is a separate entrance for business class, so I make my way over, though the rest of the business passengers, understanding Spanish, have already made their way onboard.

When I arrive in Lima, I make my way to a waiting shuttle. My group is staying in Miraflores, which is about thirty minutes south of Lima. We're only in town for the night, so our only sightseeing is on the walk to dinner. I do notice a Mcdonald's and a Starbucks, which I find a little disconcerting. One should travel to explore local culture, not bring their own culture along with them.

INTO THE WILD

After a night in Miraflores, we fly to Puerto Maldonado, our entryway into the Amazon. We're taken to a local business to leave our luggage and place what we need into smaller bags for our lodge stay. It's also where we pick up rubber boots for the impending hiking. Unfortunately, they don't have my size, so give me a pair two sizes too large, which I figure at the time would be better than two sizes too small.

The journey begins with a forty-minute motorized boat trip across the Rio Madre de Dios, whose fish population is 60% piranha. This drops us off at the beginning of a 3-mile (5 km) hike to Sandoval Lake. Being the rainy season, the hike is somewhat muddy, so I slip on my knee-high rubber boots and rain poncho, along with a tall bamboo pole for balance. The hike is very rutted in spots, so I use my pole to assist me along the sides of the trail at times. Unfortunately, my boots being two sizes too big will cause my feet to blister, which I'll discover later.

The end of the hike leads to a paddled canoe ride across Sandoval Lake. Along with the aforementioned piranha, the lake also includes electric eels and black caiman. The lodge we are staying at is a short hike from the shore along a clean and dry trail. The lodge has limited electricity and running water, though only cold water. In the heat and humidity, cold showers are not bad things. This is my first time ever sleeping beneath a mosquito net, though it's not bad. Around 4:30 in the morning comes a strong hissing sound from outside the mesh used in place of a window—I decide to let it be rather than fumbling for my flashlight in the pitch blackness of the predawn night.

MONKEYS, BIRDS, AND CAIMEN

It's an early morning rise to head back onto the lake to watch for birds and monkeys. I end up with lots of blurry photos and shots of empty branches as the birds and monkeys are quicker at jumping from branch to branch than I am at capturing them. By ten, it is starting to get rather warm, so we had back to the lodge.

In the afternoon, we head with a guide into the jungle. Around the lodge is relatively new growth, so we head into much older vegetation. Our guide is carrying a machete, and I decide to follow right behind as this seems the safest option. I don't consider that his hacking of branches right in front of me might leave one to fling itself into me, which one does. There is some blood and I'll be left with a small scar. The jungle is something that needs to be experienced firsthand—the feel of the heat and humidity on the skin, the sound of insects buzzing and humming in all directions, the sight of hundreds of varieties of flora and fauna surrounding you. I try to capture its essence with a few photos but find it an impossible task.

In the late afternoon, we head back onto the lake, searching for black caiman after sunset. I take a few last photos in the diminishing light. After dark, we head along the shore, shining flashlights along the edge, looking for the orange glow of their eyes. We do find several, though I do not attempt any photos. Sometimes one needs to sit back and enjoy the moment at hand. I'm thankful that the thousands of insects buzzing about don't seem interested in biting me. However, the blisters on my feet wish I'd not done yesterday's hike.

CUSCO BOUND

Another early morning as we have to head out of the jungle and catch a flight to Cusco, the ancient Inca capital of Peru. All night we hope that there will be no rain to further muddy the trail we'd traversed only two days before. With my rubber boots being too wide and consequently ripping up my feet on the way into the jungle, I vow to use my own boots on the way out, however slick the path. They do a good job, though they are caked in mud by the end of the hike.

I snap a few photos along a side street in Puerto Maldonado while returning my rubber boots. The airport here is a single hanger split into three sections—arrivals, departures, and security. The flight is late, as is every flight we take within Peru. Our guide tells us this is common but that the flights all eventually take off.

It is Christmas Eve, and the central plaza of Cusco is packed with merchants. I become obsessed with purchasing a poncho and finally find one at a reasonable price, just as some of us are heading back to our rooms before dinner. After dinner, I join a few in my group for drinking and dancing till four in the morning. I'm surprised how festive Christmas Eve is in Peru, though I suppose it makes sense in a Catholic country. The festivities rival New Year's Eve back home.

I'm paired this evening with one of the single women on our tour who has a propensity for vodka. I lose count after the fifth shot but am impressed with my tolerance. My maternal grandmother's family made their way from Romania to Russia and then England before ending up in America after she fell for my American grandfather. I think my Russian ancestors would proud of my vodka drinking ability.

CHRISTMAS IN CUSCO

Once the capital of the Inca Empire, Cusco is a unique mixture of Inca ruins and Catholic grandeur. Inca-built walls line the city's main streets and form the foundations for both colonial and modern structures. At the heart of Cusco is the Plaza de Armas. On the northeast side of the plaza is La Catedral, flanked by the churches of Jesús Maria and El Trifuno, the oldest church in Cusco. On the southeast side is the ornate church of La Compañia, its foundations built on the palace of Huayna Capac, the last Inca to rule an undivided, unconquered empire.

Christmas morning, my roommate and I wander the main square and surrounding areas. As my boots are still filthy from our hike out of the Amazon, I take up an offer to have them cleaned. I know I pay too much, but it's Christmas and these are the only shoes I've brought for the trip.

My roommate is a very seasoned traveler. One of his rules is to get out of tourist areas as often only a few blocks away one can find authentic experiences. Following this principle, we come across an indoor marketplace selling textiles, fruits, and meats, with very inexpensive meals in its food court. On our way back to the Plaza de Armas, we encounter one of several pageants celebrating the day. Some tourists seem to feel it is okay to walk backward in the middle of the processions with their video cameras. I resist the temptation to throw my camera at them.

After lunch, we head toward some ruins. Cusco is situated on the southeast corner of Peru's Sacred Valley, home to many ancient Inca sites. In all we visit four—this is my kind of Christmas. First up is Puka Pukara, or "red fortress," situated on a small rocky hill just 5 miles (8 km) from Cusco, which it looks down on. The fort ruins are made of large walls, terraces, and staircases. It was part of the defense of Cusco in particular and the Inca Empire in general.

Just up from here is a short hike to Tambomachay, which our guide describes as a temple dedicated to the worship of water. The site includes two clear water springs that flow through a conduit of carved stones all year round. The site's actual function is uncertain: it may have served as a military outpost guarding the approach to Cusco, as a spa resort for the Incan political elite, or as imperial baths. It could have also served a religious function since sacred water fountains have been discovered in almost all the major Incan temples, including in Pisco and Machu Picchu.

Following is Qenko, which includes an amphitheater and hall of sacrifices. Zigzagging channels, which Qenko is named for, are carved into the rocks here and were most probably used for draining llama blood in ceremonial rituals. This site leads into Saqsaywaman, known as the "House of the Sun" in the Inca era. Consisting of three platforms one on top of the other made of huge stones fit together without mortar, it was one of the most important religious complexes of its time. Today only about 20% of the original structure remains as the Spaniards used the site as a quarry after their conquest.

A FREE DAY IN RUINS

Today is a free day in Cusco. Organized options include horseback riding or rafting, but I'm not in Peru to do either. I find that two others from my group agree, so we hire a taxi in the morning and head out to three sites: Chinchero, Maras, and Moray. I'm the one with the guidebook, so I act as a guide, though all I know about the sites is what's in my guidebook. Chinchero, known as the "birthplace of the rainbow" to the Incas, combines Inca ruins and a typical Andean village. There is a colonial church just above the main village square that is built on Inca foundations. To the left of this church are extensive ruins, mainly consisting of terracing, that seem to go on for miles.

On the way to Moray is the small town of Maras. The town is well known for its salt evaporation ponds, which have been in use since Inca times. The ponds are a few miles north of the town, and there are over 5000 of them, some owned by families and others unused. The salt mines traditionally have been available to any person wishing to harvest salt. The owners of the salt ponds must be members of the community, and families that are new to the community wishing to acquire a salt pond gets the one farthest from the community.

At Moray, different levels of concentric terraces are carved into three bowls, two large and one smaller. The temperature differences in the terraces have created microclimates, similar to what is achieved in greenhouses in modern times. They are believed to have been used by the Incas to study the effects of different climatic conditions on crops. The ruins also look similar to open-pit mines. After the mining was completed, the Incas may have reinforced the walls to prevent landslides and started to grow crops on the terraces.

THE ROAD TO OLLANTAYTAMBO

In the morning, we head into the Sacred Valley on our way to Ollantaytambo. Just as we enter the valley, I take some various photos. On the way to Pisac, we make a detour to a Ccaccaccollo community supported by a foundation. While demonstrating how they achieve their natural dyes, my palm is used to develop a bright red. A faint circular red imprint remains on my palm for several days.

Pisac is divided into two distinct parts: an Inca fortress perched on a mountain spur nearly 2000 feet (600 meters) above a colonial village lying beside the Rio Urubamba. I am in heaven among the ruins and take several color and black & white shots. I also snap a few photos of the marketplace in the village. The locals of Pisac still keep many of their traditions, including their traditional attire. This is especially true of the women, who wear *lliclla* (blankets tied around their necks and used as backpacks). They also wear *polleras* (colorful and vibrant skirts) along with *jobonas* (their bright jackets).

The day ends in Ollantaytambo, an Andean town dominated by a massive Inca fortress high above. The huge, steep terraces that guard Ollantaytambo's remarkable Inca ruins mark one of the few places where the Spanish conquistadors lost a major battle, though the victory was short-lived. Though Ollantaytambo was a highly effective fortress, it also served as a temple. A ceremonial center can be found at the top of the terracing. It is an impressive site that commands respect and awe, and I am unable to truly capture this with a camera. The town itself consists of cobblestone streets and buildings built on the foundations of Inca stonework. This is also where the Incas retreated after the Spanish took Cusco.

IMAGINED REMAINS

A ninety-minute train ride from Ollantaytambo leads into Aguas Calientes, a village nestled in the deep valley beneath Machu Picchu. Also known as Machu Picchu Pueblo, Aguas Calientes derives its name from its natural thermal hot springs. The village did not exist until the railroad was built, where it first served as a center for construction workers. After the railroad opened in 1931, it took off as foreign tourists started arriving to visit the nearby ruins of Machu Picchu. What is here today came into existence as resourceful individuals set up businesses serving the tourists, primarily restaurants and small hotels. Virtually everything here is directly or indirectly serving tourists. In fact, the town has no charter, municipal government, or school.

My guidebook notes that the Puente ruins are less than a mile from our hotel. This gets me excited, so I head off on a hike to find them. After more than a mile, I come across Puente Ruinas, a train station, but no sign of ruins. I keep going, eventually coming across the back route to Machu Picchu—a steep stairway used by industrious locals trying to catch the buses going down to offer souvenirs to descending passangers. It then begins to rain and doesn't let up all night. As I'm here in the rainy season, I feel fortunate I haven't encountered any rain so far and hurry back to the hotel to dry off.

We retire early as we are going to be catching the 5:20 a.m. bus in the morning, the first one up to Machu Picchu. This will get us there before most of the tourists, who tend to start arriving around ten in the morning. We've been joined by another group from the same tour company. They are much younger and louder, and two will miss the bus in the morning. I assume they caught the next bus up.

RECENTLY UNCOVERED RUINS

Like standing on the Great Wall and being amazed to find yourself there, Machu Picchu is one of those areas that can overwhelm you. Visually stunning, historically significant, and did I mention I'm standing in the middle of it? The black & white photographer in me goes wild. I do also take several color shots. As we caught the first bus up, the ruins are at first covered in mist. Slowly the fog starts to give way, and the ruins gradually begin to appear, first as silhouettes amidst the haze, and then details start to emerge. I wonder if Hiram Bingham had a similar experience in 1911.

After a two-hour guided tour of the main sites, two of us decide to hike out to the Inca drawbridge during our free time. Someone coming from that area tells us it is only five to ten minutes to reach it. After twenty minutes of hiking a narrow, slippery path along the edge of a steep canyon wall, I consult my guidebook to find that it is indeed a twenty-minute hike. Another five or so minutes, and we finally reach the bridge. It's an underwhelming site in part because no one is allowed to get close to it after an incident involving careless tourists years before. So, it's now just a view across a chasm to a few pieces of wood connecting a break in a path along a cliff wall.

Back at the main site, several llamas and alpacas can be found around the Hut of the Caretaker of the Funerary Rock. This also seems to be an area that some like to attempt meditation or even yoga. As the heat is increasing along with the crowds, I decide head back into town. Before leaving, I do get my passport stamped through the little blink-and-you'll-miss-it doorway near the exit.

CUSCO REDUX

In the afternoon, we return to Cusco for one last day before heading to Puno. My roommate and I have become known as the "Crazy Californians" by the others in our group for our love of hiking up to most anything. Living up to our nickname, we head up toward a church we hadn't been to in our prior visit. Tibet must have been good for my lungs as the elevation hasn't hit me yet. One in our group was hit as soon as we arrived in Cusco the first time and barely recovered in time to head into the Sacred Valley.

The next morning, we fly to Puno, with an elevation of around 12,500 feet (3800 meters). I notice that I start to feel occasional heart palpitations and shortness of breath at this elevation as I wander around town. There is not much to Puno itself—it is a port town leading to Lake Titicaca, the highest navigable lake in the world. It is somewhat utilitarian in design, making one long for the freedom of the sea. Puno is positioned between the shores of Lake Titicaca and the mountains surrounding it. As such, there are less than two miles of flat land between the coasts and the foothills, which has caused the city to expand upwards onto the hillsides.

For New Year's Eve, we participate in a shamanic ceremony that includes a ritual cleansing, prayer, and blessing. It's quite the contrast to my Christmas Eve spent dancing and downing vodka shots. As part of the ritual, we're each granted three wishes, though I honestly don't have anything to wish for—I'm quite content where I am and with what I've got. Maybe I can cash them in when I'm not feeling so satisfied.

FLOATING ISLANDS

The following morning, we head out early onto Lake Titicaca. Here I take a few photos on our way to the Uros Islands, which are made entirely from totora reeds. In fact, the lives of the inhabitants of these artificial islands are dependent upon the reed beds they live among. Totora reeds were initially used centuries ago to build these islands on Lake Titicaca by the Uro-Aymara, who made their home on the lake. The local's boats are also made from these reeds, which they use for fishing. Even some of their handcrafts are made from totora reeds, and the welcoming people of this community offer their work to visitors as a souvenir of their visit.

It's about a half hour's motorized boat ride from Puno to reach the floating islands of the Uros community. These reed islands were begun centuries ago in an attempt by the Uros to isolate themselves from the more aggressive Collas and Incas. I tower over the locals, one of which asks my name, and then uses it to call me over to her stall of handicrafts after a brief tour around the island. It's a good gimmick, and I purchase a small tapestry from her. We then head out on a reed boat toward another, much larger island that includes a bar, restaurant, mini-market, and lodge.

Back on the motorized boat, it's another three hours to Isla Taquile, which has been inhabited for thousands of years and presently has a population of about 2000 (not counting the tourists). Once we reach the island, we take the back route up to the top, which is longer than the main route but far less steep and far less traveled. After lunch, we return to port. It's been a long day—even our guide sleeps on the way back to Puno.

BACK TO LIMA

Our flight back to Lima doesn't leave till the afternoon, so the Crazy Californians decide to spend part of their last morning in Puno ascending Mirador de Kuntur Wasi, also known as Condor Hill. We're already at 12,500 feet, so what're another 600 to 700 feet? The metal condor at the top of the hill serves both as a reminder of the community's Andean heritage and as one of the most striking vantage points to view the city and the lake. The monument stands at the end of a 620-step staircase, and I must pause a few times to catch my breath at this altitude.

As expected, our flight is delayed, though always listed as being "on time." In the morning, having not seen much of Lima, two of us share a taxi downtown before sharing another taxi to the airport. As we are both carrying all our luggage, we decide on Lima's Plaza de Armas as a central location where one of us can wander and take photos while the other guards the bags. I head off first. The plaza consists of both a cathedral and the Palacio de Gobierno, complete with armed guards and armored vehicles. When it's time for us to depart, two police officers patrolling the plaza flag down and negotiate a taxi to the airport for us. I last see my companion as she's hurriedly trying to find the gate for her already boarding plane.

Both flights home are uneventful, though security is tight, and carry-ons are searched at the gate in San Salvador. Security is also tight leaving baggage claim in Los Angeles. As I'm coming off a plane from El Salvador, wearing a poncho and carrying an Israeli Mossad tactical duffle bag, I figure I'll be stopped for sure for questioning, but there is no problem. I'm back home and back to work in a few days.

CLOSING THOUGHTS

Peru and Machu Picchu were all that I had expected. I am very happy we got up early to catch the 5:20 a.m. bus to Machu Picchu as the area began to flood with tourists in the late morning, and this was during the off-season. I'm also glad I chose to climb some of Mount Machu Picchu instead of Huayna Picchu, which allows for the classic view of the ruins with Huayna Picchu in the background. While I did see one girl take some time to meditate and become one with the environment, dozens of others were walking around yakking on their cell phones. I again resisted the urge to throw my camera at them.

Now that I've been to a few busy cities around the world, I've come to realize that nothing seems to have the right of way and that the lines in the road are only suggestions. The taxi ride to and from the Lima airport would undoubtedly take a few years from most anyone's life. So will trying to cross certain intersections. I'm learning to just move forward and leave it to the locals to avoid a collision.

I've also come to love the way my name is pronounced in Latin America: Jeremy becomes "Yeramie" and Jeremiah becomes "Yeramias." My parents named me Jeremiah figuring people would shorten it to Jeremy, which they do. However, I don't think they realized the difficulty some would have in spelling either. My favorite variations are Jerome for Jeremy (this was by a family friend) and Jaramaya for Jeremiah (this one from my own college district). Most commonly, I get Jeramy or Jeremie. To her credit, a cashier in a fast-food restaurant in Cusco, who didn't speak English, spelled it correctly.

Jul. 2008 – *Guatemala and Honduras*

I was thinking of a trip to Thailand during Spring Break this year but figured it was a bit far to go for only a week. So I started looking closer to home. The company I had taken my Copper Canyon, Mexico trip with also offered a two-week trip to Guatemala and Honduras. I'd enjoyed my prior trip with them, so I moved my travel plans to summer where I'd have more time. Like the Mexico trip, it's a full bus and I'm seated with the only other solo traveler on tour again, though this time she's a pastry chef from Montreal with a wonderful French accent. Better yet, she's not trying to help the locals find Jesus.

GUNS AND BUDDHAS

To reach Guatemala City, I fly through Houston, where I have a five-and-a-half-hour layover. After three hours, I'm going crazy, then notice a flight leaving two hours before mine. I'm able to get on it and cut my layover short, thankfully. On the flight are two pairs of church groups, one in matching red shirts and the other in matching orange shirts, each with a passage from the New Testament on it. I notice that while the leaders of the orange group sit with their flock in coach, the leaders of the red group are sitting in first class. Their group must receive better donations.

We visit the Ixchel Museum in the morning, named after the Maya goddess of fertility and weaving. After perusing the museum, I explore a bit of its outskirts. Behind the museum, after a ramp and a ladder, is a narrow trail that I am tempted by, but it is rather steep, and it is starting to rain, so I decide to leave it unexplored.

The hotel we are staying at is stunning and situated atop a shopping center. In the afternoon, I explore a bit of the mall and somehow end up ordering two lunches. Either my Spanish is worse than I thought, or I looked famished. I'm going to go with the former. After lunch, I come across a store selling firearms beside another store with a selection of Buddhist statues. That's one approach to dualism, I suppose.

Back in my room, somewhat sleep-deprived and a little restless, I pass some time trying to take some creative photos through my door's peephole. I also can't resist watching *Predator* dubbed in Spanish.

TEXTILES, MASKS, AND STATUES

On our way to Lake Atitlán, we make a stop in Katok to stretch our legs. While there, I decide to get in a little black & white photo practice while the others are shopping. I never set out with a particular souvenir in mind and certainly know I won't find it in typical souvenir shops set up for tourists. Nothing against those buying T-shirts or refrigerator magnets; I just know they aren't for me. This is the first of four long travel days, which will span every other day, so any stop is appreciated.

Before stopping at the marketplace in Chichicastenango, we have lunch. Then it's on to market day. Chichicastenango hosts market days on Thursdays and Sundays where vendors sell a vast array of items, including handicrafts, food, pottery, condiments, medicinal plants, candles, grindstones, pigs, chickens, and machetes. I snap some photos of various wears as we head toward Santo Tomas Church, built-in 1540. K'iche' Maya priests still use the church for their rituals, and each of the eighteen stairs that lead up to the church represents one month of the Maya calendar year.

We then head into Panajachel, where we will take a thirty-minute boat ride to Santa Catarina Palopó on the shores of Lake Atitlán, where our next hotel lies. By now, it is raining, so it is a dash from the boat to the hotel. We are surrounded by the San Pedro, Toliman, and Atitlán volcanoes, which we will get a better view of in the morning when we head out by sea to reach the village of Santiago Atitlán.

CREATED BY FIRE

In the morning, we head down to the pier before embarking on an hour-long boat ride to Santiago Atitlán, squeezed between the volcanoes of Tolimán and San Pedro and home to a large arts and crafts scene. I am fortunate that I have never suffered from seasickness and enjoy darting about the ship taking assorted photos. I'm reminded of the time my father didn't want to get on the ferry from Seattle to Victoria, British Columbia and then ended up spending the whole time riding the waves on the bow of the ship.

Once docked, we make our way into the village. Most of its residents are indigenous Mayans. It was the capital of the Tz'utujil people in pre-Columbian times when its name was Chuitinamit. Today, it is geared toward tourists. Its main road is essentially one shop after another, all seemingly selling the same things. We stop at a cantina for a drink, where I try a Guatemalan beer. I've picked up a habit of trying local beers, though I never drink them back home.

We end our trip with a visit to the Iglesia Parroquial Santiago Apostol, constructed between 1572 and 1581. Along its walls are wooden statues of the saints, each with new clothes made by local women every year. These saints are quite animated; there is even one in a very striking Elvis pose. At the front of the church stand three altarpieces symbolizing the three volcanoes around Santiago, which are believed to protect the town. The central one was subtly changed from a conventional European vision of heaven to a more Maya representation of a sacred mountain with two church members climbing toward a sacred cave. Inside is also a statue of God, which is rare to find. He can be recognized by the triangle affixed behind his head.

THE ROAD LESS TRAVELLED

We return to our hotel for a rest, and after a few hours, we head back out on the boat. This time we are sailing into Panajachel, which is again filled with shop after shop ostensibly selling the same things. However, I pick up a wooden bowl because of the incredible blue it possesses at its base. I employ my bartering lesson adopted after Tibet— I ask the price and, finding it too high, walk away. This leads to the seller chasing after me with a much more reasonable price that we agree upon.

In the morning, we head out on our next long travel day, this time into Honduras. Before we go, we stop for one last view of Lake Atitlán and its surrounding volcanoes. Then the adventure begins. An hour into the drive, we discover that a mudslide blocks the road, so we must head back to where we'd just come from to try a second route. Less than an hour on that route, and there's another mudslide. So, we end up on a lesser-used southern route known for bandits that like to hold up tour buses. We set off on this road only after our guide has secured an armed vehicle to follow us to the border.

Several hours behind schedule, we finally make it to the Honduran border. It is a very smooth border crossing, but we are informed that the bridge just beyond has been washed out. Our guide and driver have a frantic discussion in Spanish before yet another alternate route is found. Thanks to some skillful driving, we finally arrive at our destination. The good news after such a long day? The hotel happens to employ one of the world's most beautiful bartenders, and a drink or two is certainly in order.

THE TWO COPANS

There are two Copáns in Honduras, the ruins and the town, confusingly named Copán Ruinas. We are staying in the town and head into the ruins in the morning, less than a mile to the east of town. Discovered in 1570 by Diego García de Palacio, the ruins of Copán, one of the most significant sites of Mayan civilization, were not excavated until the 19th century. Its ruined citadel and commanding public squares reveal three main stages of development before the city was abandoned in the early 10th century. The Plaza of the Hieroglyphic Staircase, for instance, has a monumental staircase. On its 30-foot-wide steps, there are more than 1,250 individual glyphs, constituting the longest known Mayan inscription. After the city was abandoned, it was swallowed by the jungle, which helped its conservation.

The ruins at Copán are essentially divided into two sections. The lower section, where one first enters, includes many stelae, a small pyramid, and several relatively low structures. We are told that 85% of the stelae that we see are original, the remaining 15% having been replaced with replicas. The second section requires a bit of a climb and includes the Acropolis and much taller structures.

The stelae that have been replaced by replicas can be found in the adjoining Museo de Escultura, which requires one to enter through the mouth of a snake and follow a sinuous tunnel to reach the museum. I'm not too fond of snakes but brave the entrance anyway. I am rewarded with full-scale replica of the Rosalila Temple, discovered in nearly perfect condition by archaeologists in 1989.

SINGLE-HANDED PHOTOS

After returning to the hotel, a group of us decide to go horseback riding. At first, it was going to be zip-lining, but we were told that it was not safe after so much rain, so horses it is. A van picks us up and takes us to a location where we can saddle up. The horses' owner takes one look at me and returns with a horse at least one hand taller than the rest. I begin taking single-handed photos while my other hand grips the reins. I haven't been on a horse in years and do not trust myself to try any double-handed photos while in transit.

The small ceremonial site of Los Sapos, located across the river from Copán, is believed to be tied to ancient Maya birthing and fertility practices. There is a very small and minimally excavated site located here. You can see some stone carvings of *sapos*, or frogs, and the carved figure of a pregnant woman. In addition, the site features the exposed foundations of a few large structures.

Upon arrival in Los Sapos, we are inundated with little girls selling flowers made from corn husks. One of them, Helen, knows some English and ends up in several photos. She also starts taking pictures with one of my group's cameras, which leads another girl, Araceli, to want to give it a try. I also end up buying Araceli's flower and ride back down with it in my left-front pocket.

My horse seems fine letting every other horse pass him until he notices he's last, then he speeds up to get back into the lead only to start the process all over again. This makes conversing with others challenging as he'll just bolt ahead when he notices his position without warning. I suspect he doesn't get out much.

ANOTHER ROAD TO RUINS

We begin our third long travel today heading back into Guatemala and then north to Tikal. We will be staying on Laguna Petenchel, a small lake east of Santa Elena. Tikal itself is about another hour's drive further into the jungle. Unlike in Peru, no piranha this time, though there are crocodiles.

For lunch, we stop in Rio Dulce, lined with yachts from around the world. There are also some turtles in a pond behind the restaurant. Otherwise, it is an uneventful day. In the morning, on the way to Tikal, we stop to get a look at Lago de Petén Itzá, the third largest lake in Guatemala after Izabal and Atitlán. Then it's on to our hotel before an early morning visit to Tikal, founded around 700 BCE.

Unlike most other Mayan sites, Tikal is situated deep in the jungle. Walking from one area to another often requires one to pass beneath the dense canopy of the rain forest. It is a bit of a walk before reaching the first pyramid, but the first glimpse of Temple I is awe-inspiring. It is situated at the east end of the Gran Plaza, home to Temple II and the Acropolis del Norte. Temple II is climbable, so I climb it with one of my group. It is a steep climb, so on our way down, she asks me to go first as my height will prevent her from seeing just how steep it is.

Up until now, the path is well maintained, and the jungle is kept at bay, but to reach the next area, it is necessary to go into the jungle. Here we catch a glimpse of Temple III, along with various other ruins. But the hallmark of any visit to Tikal is Temple IV, the largest of the pyramids at 144 feet (44 meters) in height. The view from its top is exquisite.

MONOLITHS AND MOSQUITOS

In the morning, we head back south toward our final destination: Antigua. Along the way, we stop in Quiriguá, home to many zoomorphic figures and the world's tallest stelae, which record Mayan history. At the heart of Quiriguá is its Great Plaza, the largest known public space in the entire Maya area. The immense complexes set out around the Great Plaza, the Ceremonial Plaza, and the Plaza of the Temple are notable for the complexity of their structure, including a highly elaborate system of pyramids, terraces, and staircases.

Our last long travel day passes much quicker than the previous ones, and we find ourselves at our hotel at a decent hour. Like much of Antigua, our hotel is colonial in style, so I pass some time before dinner taking a few photos and familiarizing myself with the grounds. One of our group thinks her room might be haunted, but I get no such sense from my room. Given the atrocities committed by Spain throughout the region, I can only imagine most everything here has the potential to be haunted.

In the morning, we head to the Museo del Café. Not too interested in an elaborate explanation of the history and processing of coffee, I break off from my group to take some photos, mostly in black & white for some reason. Must be inspired by the dark roasts. I do return to purchase some coffee in the ever-present gift shop. I am a latecomer to coffee but have grown to appreciate Central and South American beans. My parents both drank coffee growing up, but they preferred a weak roast that smelled much better than it tasted. In grad school, I was introduced to the French press, and I have not looked back since.

IN THE DETAILS

The coffee museum is followed by a visit to La Merced Church, which stands out for its Baroque-style architecture. The building has a lovely facade with decorative elements set in relief and the arresting yellow color of its main walls accompanied by white plaster sculptures. The church has its origins in a monastery that existed from the 17th century. After an earthquake in 1773, important statuary was moved to a new congregation. However, La Merced Church's community moved back to the original building in the mid-19th century.

This is followed by a walk down to Las Capuchinas Convent, inaugurated in 1736 by nuns from Madrid. It was also seriously damaged by the earthquake in 1773 and subsequently abandoned. Restoration began in 1943 and continue into the present day. They say that God is in the details, and I become a little obsessed with the architectural details myself. I could spend all day here exploring every nook and cranny. Still, time is limited, so I pacify myself by taking as many color and (mostly) black & white photos as I can.

After lunch, I set out to explore Antigua. The city was founded in 1543 and named Santiago de los Caballeros. For more than 200 years, it served as the seat of the military governor of the Spanish colony of Guatemala. This large region included almost all of present-day Central America and the southernmost state of Mexico, Chiapas. Three volcanoes encompass the city, and its streets are designed on a grid system, making it easy to navigate. Should one get lost, they can look for Arco de Santa Catalina, one of the few original constructions to withstand the 1773 earthquake and a popular meeting place.

GOING AND COMING

While I begin on side streets, I soon find myself in the central part of town. Due to the numerous earthquakes in the area over the centuries, Antigua is a mix of restored colonial architecture and ruins. In other words, my kind of place. The route I am taking passes several churches, so I have no complaints. While I am not a religious person, I have always admired the beauty found in sacred sites. One can also not underestimate the impact religion has had on shaping the modern world, especially in Central and South America.

After lunch, one of my group has asked me to help her find the hotel she will be transferring to as she will be spending a few extra days in Antigua to take a cooking class and climb a volcano. As for me, in the morning, it's back to the airport to return for a few days at home before setting off again. If I had to do it over, I would have stayed a few more days in Antigua, then spent a few days at my cousin's house in Costa Rica before heading up to Alajuela and the institute I will be visiting upon my return.

As it turns out, it's fortunate that I did return home. While I am currently living in an apartment, I have always loved townhouses ever since visiting a famous friend's townhouse in Hollywood. Mind you, I could never afford the townhouse he had, but I do come across a new development closer to home that I tour, find the unit I love, and put a deposit down on. So, while in Costa Rica, I will shift from thinking about souvenirs to buying nicer items to add to my new home.

Aug. 2008 – *Costa Rica*

After a few days off, I'm again heading to Central America. This time it's Los Angeles to Dallas, then Dallas to San Jose. I am not thrilled to be flying through Dallas as I have never had a flight there ever leave on time or from its original gate. This time proves to be the same, though the problems start in Los Angeles. While I watched the cleaning crew disembark our plane ten minutes prior, an announcement comes that there is a delay while the aircraft is being cleaned. Noticing that the right engine cover is open, either the airline employs very thorough cleaning crews, or it's an engine problem causing the delay. Ten minutes later comes the announcement that it's an engine problem. We finally set off an hour late. The gate doesn't change in Dallas as it's the same plane, though its departure is also delayed.

WORK AND RAIN

Late into Costa Rica, I meet my host family after Customs and Immigration. I have never lived with a host family before and am not sure what to expect. My poor Spanish skills are also a concern. As for accommodations, it's an old, lumpy mattress, one working electrical outlet, and very dim lighting. In the morning, I'll learn that I'm also in for cold showers all week.

As this is essentially a business trip, the morning finds me off to the Instituto de Cultura y Lengua Costarricense, or ICLC for short. After our first workshop, I take a few photos of the rolling campus, which is quite nice. After our second workshop, I note the dark clouds growing, which are soon followed by rain. Lots of rain. Lunch was to be followed by a tour of Grecia, but the rain and wind are too heavy, and we hold up in the restaurant until our host families arrive to take us home.

I learn upon my return that it is their son's birthday, so we celebrate by playing video games for a few hours (I don't understand any of the instructions—I just wing it and continuously look for patterns of right and wrong behavior) and then we have pizza and cola for dinner. Feeling bad about not having a gift, I quickly draw him a cartoon of himself that he seems to like—good thing for simple pleasures.

After he's gone to bed, I find myself tutoring his mother in mathematics, ranging from beginning algebra to trigonometry. It is very interesting trying to explain how to factor using my broken Spanish, but we seem to do okay. A well-placed Spanish-to-English dictionary between us is referred to often.

MBA, ANYONE?

Two more workshops this morning at the institute. During our break, three of us book a tour for Friday, our only free day during the week. Before lunch, we also visit a public high school, whose students I may be instructing next summer if my idea for the institute works out. While the others in my group are here to try to restart a study abroad program, I am here to push a different idea. The principal seems to like my idea very much, and we have a photo of us taken shaking hands with the Costa Rican flag behind us.

After lunch, we head over to the INCAE Business School, the number two business school in Central America (and number ten in the world). INCAE is an acronym for *Instituto Centroamericano de Administración de Empresas*, or "Central American Institute of Business Administration." The campus is built on an old golf course, so the landscaping is remarkable. The classrooms are also high-tech, with instructors provided with everything that they could need. I half-jokingly inquire if they need a mathematics professor and get an affirmative response. If I could stay in one of the resort-like houses they have for students, I would seriously consider it.

Back with my host family, it's more video game playing with the son before dinner and mathematics tutoring after dinner. Beforehand, I walk around my neighborhood in Carrillos Bajo and snap a few photos, beginning with one of the house I'm staying at. Before I head out, I promise my host family that I will not wander too far as they seem to have safety concerns. I take just my camera and promise to be return in twenty minutes.

LEYDI AND THE TRAMP

Students who study at the ICLC have classes in the morning but often have free time in the afternoon and we are being shown some of the options they have for sightseeing and practicing their new language skills. We start in Carrillos Alto, where we visit a clinic some ICLC students have interned at, while others have been treated there. We are then on our way to downtown Alajuela, the birthplace of Juan Santamaría, the national hero of Costa Rica and the figure who gives the name to the country's main international airport.

Then it's a visit to the Sr. Y Sra. Ese wood factory, whose grounds are picturesque and some of its creations are exceptional. We tour the facilities wearing protective eye wear and gasmasks due to the sawdust in the air and some of the lacquers they use before making our way to the gift shop, where most of my purchases for this trip are made. I'm in full new house mode, finding objects I think will work well in the townhouse.

After lunch, it's a visit to INBio Park, a private research and biodiversity management center established in 1989 to support efforts to gather knowledge on Costa Rica's biological diversity and promote its sustainable use. It is run by the National Biodiversity Institute (*Instituto Nacional de Biodiversidad*, or INBio). It is part museum, part educational center, and part nature park. Our guide, Leydi, leads us down a trail that includes both a rain forest and a dry forest, among several other diverse ecosystems. There is also a series of playful animal sculptures donated by one of Costa Rica's premier artists, José Sancho. Unshaven and damp from the humidity, I'm starting to remember what I don't like about rain forests.

COFFEE, SULFUR, AND LOTS OF WATER

Our free day is supposed to begin at 7:10 a.m. in front of the Juan Santamaria Monument in Alajuela. However, by 7:30, no one has arrived the pick us up. Just as we start to realize that we have no idea who to call or what to do, the shuttle arrives, and we are off to a coffee plantation for breakfast and a tour. Of course, here in Costa Rica, they claim to have the best coffee, just as in Guatemala, you are told the same about their coffee. The coffee plantation I visited in Guatemala told us that Costa Rican coffee is better known because they are better at publicity. Don't tell them, but I find the Costa Rican coffee tends to be smoother.

Then it's a relatively short drive up to Poás Volcano, considered to possess the largest active crater in the world. The crater is shrouded in clouds that are saturated with sulfur. Every so often, the clouds lift, and one of the crater's two lakes is revealed. It is a waiting game that I am willing to pay for a good photo, though the sulfur can get a little intense at times. Note to self: Bring a face mask for future volcanic visits.

On our way to the La Paz Waterfall Gardens in Vara Blanca, we stop to take in a good view of Costa Rica's central valley, where my stay has been focused. Soon after, we encounter a sloth hanging from an overhead line. Everyone is out of the van we're traveling in and snapping photos. I wonder what the sloth is thinking.

La Paz Waterfall Gardens Nature Park is a privately owned and managed ecological attraction that opened in the fall of 2000, following the construction of the hiking trails, butterfly observatory, and reception area. We begin our visit by entering a bird-watching area. This is followed by a stop at the butterfly observatory. Then it is on to the waterfalls. First up is El Templo, followed by Magia Blanca, the largest and most powerful of the falls. Lastly, we catch a view of the La Paz waterfall on our way out.

To end our day, it's a boat ride on the Sarapiquí River. The area around the river is primarily lowland tropical rainforest, having lush vegetation with a large variety of plant, animal, and insect life. We're on the lookout for plants and animals, and the insects are on the lookout for us. Along with tourism, the river is also a local trading artery. Around the river are plantations of coffee, sugar cane, bananas, and cocoa trees.

It's an extremely long bus ride, including two transfers, back to Alajuela, followed by dinner and a taxi home. It was a full day of sightseeing I would have normally broken into a few days, but our return flight is in the morning, and this was our only free day. I feel bad arriving so late back at my host family's house as I had no way of letting them know how late I would be.

In the morning, my host family takes me to the airport where I fly into Miami before heading back to Los Angeles. As I did not receive an exit stamp when leaving Guatemala, my passport makes it seem as if I have been in Central American for longer than I have. The Customs official in Miami seems unsure how I was able to do it while carrying only a small bag carryon. "Checked bag?" he inquires. "No, just this one," I reply. He seems impressed.

Jun. 2009 – *Spain, Portugal, and Morocco*

Though I'd only started seriously traveling a few years prior by this point, I was hooked. My travels gained in frequency, and I started thinking about where to go next before even setting off. I planned to set foot on each of the seven continents before turning forty in two years, or at least the six inhabited ones. This thought very much influenced the choice of this trip, as it would get me up to five continents. This was not the only deciding factor, of course. First and foremost, I had always wanted to see Morocco. Along with Egypt and Tunisia, it was high on my list of countries to visit and would also mark my first Muslim country. Secondly, a friend of mine, who has been all over Europe, never misses the chance to return to Spain and Portugal, so I would like to see what drew him.

INTO THE LABYRINTH

To reach Madrid, I fly from Los Angeles through London (Heathrow). Once at Heathrow, I discover two things: (1) My flight to Madrid is still in Madrid, and (2) Heathrow is one of the most confusing airports I have ever been to. After a bus, a train, and several escalators and elevators providing numerous elevation changes, I survive the labyrinth and reach my gate. Sometime later, my flight to Madrid finally takes off.

My maternal grandmother was British, and I am sorry to say this is my first time in London, and then only as a layover. I do plan to leave the airport someday, though right now, Europe isn't high on my list (writes the guy headed to Spain). I've always felt Europe, especially Western Europe, is somewhere that can be explored when one is older. This doesn't mean it couldn't or shouldn't be explored when younger, just that I feel I can postpone a visit in favor of more remote and demanding locations for now.

Once in Madrid, I settle into my room and then head out for a local dinner and to the nearby market for some provisions. My improved Spanish helps in both endeavors. In the morning, it's a trip to Toledo, encircled on three sides by the Tagus River. Toledo was known as the "city of three cultures" in the Middle Ages, as it was a place where Christian, Muslim, and Jewish communities peacefully coexisted. The old part of the city reminds me of Antigua, my favorite city in Guatemala. Given its history, it's not surprising that its star attractions include horseshoe-arched mosques, Sephardic synagogues, and one of Spain's premier Gothic cathedrals scattered around its dense historical center.

BULLS AND RAIN

A tour of Madrid starts with a stop at the Plaza de Toros de Las Ventas. Inaugurated in 1931, this famous bullring seats 25,000 and has also been used for concerts. This is followed by a square that features a monument to Miguel de Cervantes Saavedra and his most famous creation: Don Quixote. While here, I snap some assorted photos of the area. Next, it's on to the Royal Palace, but it starts to rain heavily, so I'm only able to sneak in two photos before heading back to the shelter of my hotel.

In the morning, we begin the journey west toward Portugal. On the way to Coimbra is a stop in Avila, most known for its medieval city walls constructed of brown granite in 1090. In addition to the walls, Avila asserts that it is one of the towns with the highest number of Romanesque and Gothic churches per capita in Spain. Both make Avila a must-see in my book, and I get in many photos.

Next is Salamanca, which lies on a mountain by the Tormes River. Here I find an Internet café to check in with friends and family back home, snap a few photos, and chose a location for lunch based on the cute redhead welcoming patrons outside. Salamanca is one of Spain's most important university cities, attracting thousands of international students each year. As a college professor, I've always enjoyed visiting university towns. They tend to possess the same youthful energy one finds on campus. The city is also home to the University of Salamanca, founded in 1218, making it the oldest university in Spain and the third oldest western university.

THE WRITING ON THE WALL

The evening finds me in Coimbra, home to the University of Coimbra, the oldest academic institution in the Portuguese-speaking world and one of the oldest in Europe. In addition to the university, the city still contains many archaeological structures dating back to the Roman era, including its well-preserved aqueduct and cryptoporticus—a covered passageway built to create an artificial platform over which the city's Forum Page could be built. Similarly, buildings from the period when Coimbra was the capital of Portugal in the tenth and eleventh centuries remain.

In the morning, I head into Coimbra proper. It's a holiday in Portugal, so foot traffic is light as most shops are closed. This makes for some nice solitary photography. I've always enjoyed taking photos with no one in them, which can especially be challenging in Europe with its throngs of tourists in the summer, so this is an unexpected delight. There is also some interesting graffiti to be found, though I can only infer the meaning of the words of those that come with accompanying drawings.

Next is a visit to the Mosteiro Santa Maria da Vitoria, more commonly known as the Batalha Monastery, a Dominican monastery in the town of Batalha. The monastery was built to thank the Virgin Mary for the Portuguese victory over the Castilians in the battle of Aljubarrota in 1385 and was completed in 1517. Its ornate limestone exterior has turned a yellow ochre over time. It features pinnacles and parapets, flying buttresses, and balustrades, along with late-Gothic carved windows. Its remarkable main doorway's layered arches are filled with apostles, angels, saints, and prophets.

MORE VIRGINS THAN ONE CAN COUNT

"Our Lady of Fatima" is the title given to the apparition of the Virgin Mary that appeared to three shepherd children at Fatima on the 13th day of six consecutive months in 1917, starting in May. Since then, the location has become an attraction for pilgrims and the devout. There is something else that makes Fatima unique, though. While in Catholicism it is a custom to burn a candle for your loved ones, in Fatima, not only are regular candles burnt, but also candles in the shape of body parts. For instance, one burns a candle in the form of a leg to pray for one's mother who just had her leg broken. While the devout are going about doing this (and the tourists are hitting the abundant souvenir shops featuring the Virgin Mary in every incarnation imaginable), I snap a few photos and then head for another Internet café.

Watching some of the pilgrims, I'm reminded of my time in Lhasa, where I also saw many pilgrims. Here they crawl on their knees toward their destination rather than spin prayer wheels and slowly walk clockwise around a temple. I do notice some are wearing knee pads, which seems like cheating to me.

That night we arrive in Lisbon. I head out with a leggy blonde from Nebraska and a middle-aged Brit from my group into the heart of the city via the Metro. After several wrong turns, we end up in a part of town filled with hippies, transients, and prostitutes. I get in a few assorted photos while also trying to keep an eye on my belongings. Eventually, we come across trolley tracks and follow them back to a better part of town. As the two Americans, we decide to let the Brit choose where to head for dinner, and he surprisingly chooses McDonald's.

TOWERS, BEACHES, AND MOUNTAINS

The following morning finds us at Belem Tower, built in the early 16th century in the Portuguese late-Gothic style, the Manueline, to commemorate Vasco da Gama's expedition. It is often seen as a symbol of Europe's Age of Discoveries and has become synonymous with Lisbon and Portugal. Nearby is the Monument to the Discoveries, located along the river where ships departed to explore and trade with India and the Orient. It celebrates the Portuguese who took part in the Age of Discovery of the 15th and 16th centuries. Also nearby is the Hieronymites Monastery, a grand, ornate structure that was historically associated with early sailors and explorers. I'm noticing a pattern here.

The afternoon finds me in Cascais, a former fishing village turned resort for both locals and foreigners. I take a few photos downtown before finding an Irish pub, where I stop for a pint of Guinness (properly poured, I might add). I then head toward the beach, where I snap a few more photos. I've never been much of a beach person, so finding creative ways to shoot is challenging as I also try to stay out of the sun.

Next up is another resort location, Sintra, which is overlooked by the Castle of the Moors and has been a favorite of Portuguese royalty through the years. Its medieval National Palace still looks very much like it must have in the 16th century and is notable for its two enormous conical chimneys, which have become the town's hallmark. After exploring this, I wander about the city a bit before stopping for a coffee and a danish. Then it's back to Lisbon, where I spend a less adventurous night than the night before.

DONS JUAN AND GIOVANNI WALK INTO A BAR

The following day finds me in Seville, home to many literary characters, including Don Juan, Don Giovanni, and Bizet's Carmen. After settling into my room, I head out once more with the leggy blonde to explore the city. Of course, we take a wrong turn and get lost, though we do eventually find the Cathedral of Seville, which was our intent. A rather burly fellow at the door spots my camera and points to an icon of a camera with a slash through it. I think it means no flash photography, but I don't want to risk angering the large man, so I put my camera away before entering.

Next is the city of Italica, founded in 206 BCE by the Roman general Publius Cornelius Scipio Africanus in order to settle Roman soldiers wounded in the Battle of Ilipa. Italica was the first Roman settlement in Spain and the first Roman city outside of Italy. It was also the birthplace of three emperors, including Trajan and Hadrian, becoming an extravagant urban center under the reign of Hadrian. It is a very well-preserved Roman city with cobbled Roman streets and mosaic floors. Small baths and a theater are some of the oldest remains, both built before Hadrian.

We then return to Seville and do a proper tour of its cathedral. No burly fellow outside this time, so I take some photos inside and out. At the time of its completion in the 1500s, it supplanted the Hagia Sophia as the largest cathedral in the world. It also serves as the burial site of Christopher Columbus and his son Diego. The tour complete, I snap a few more photos of town while heading back to my hotel for a much-needed siesta against the afternoon heat.

SOUTH TO NORTH

After my siesta (sometimes it's good to go native), I head back into town to stretch my legs and snap several more photos. Just as I start to consider heading somewhere for dinner, I run into the leggy blonde, and we head out together. While searching for a location she'd seen earlier in the day, we come across the city's walls, which first fortified the city in 1135 under Almoravid sovereignty. Just as we're about to call it quits, we find the pizzeria she had in mind and order a five-cheese pizza. As it turns out, five cheeses were one too many as one of them tastes off.

The morning starts the journey south to Morocco. We take the ferry from Algeciras to Ceuta, an autonomous territory of Spain located on the North African side of the Strait of Gibraltar. So, we've crossed from Europe to Africa and still haven't left Spain. It's about a five-minute drive to the official border crossing into Morocco, where my passport is stamped and a "policy number" is assigned, required by hotels and campsites.

Our first stop in Morocco is Tétouan, which lies along the Martial Valley and is one of the two main ports of Morocco on the Mediterranean Sea. Tétouan is a renowned multicultural center, with its medina being a UNESCO World Heritage site since 1997. Unfortunately, we're only here for a pit stop and on the outskirts of town. So, I snap a few photos while others use the restroom and then grab a snack from a small shop for the road. To pass the time on the winding road to Fez, I take a few photos through the bus window, complete with window smudges and reflections. I've made it to my fifth continent in three years.

ANOTHER LABYRINTH

The evening finds us in Fez. Upon arrival, I go into town to change some money and buy some rations, finding my limited high school French coming in handy. After dinner, I escort the leggy blonde so that she can do the same. She is wearing shorts and a strappy top and receives many damning looks, especially from the local women. In fact, the shop owner won't even look at her, so I conduct the entire sale with him on her behalf. Figuring, at this rate, she may end up being stoned and I'll be arrested for being in the company of a salacious woman, I suggest a long skirt and sleeves for her for the rest of our stay in Morocco. Her fiancé, a tour guide currently in Russia, later thanks me for the suggestion.

If Heathrow is a modern-day labyrinth, then the medina of Fez is a much older one—delve deep enough and one can probably still find a Minotaur. Filled with compact, winding streets, indescribable scents, and cries of "Balak! Balak!" when an unyielding donkey is approaching, it is reminiscent of the Amazon in that it is nearly impossible to be put into words—it really needs to be experienced. From tanneries to rug shops, you can find and smell it here.

We are given some sprigs of mint to place under our noses while visiting a tannery as the smell can be overwhelming otherwise. Fez's tanneries are composed of various stone vessels filled with a wide range of dyes and various liquids spread out in the open air. Dozens of men, many waist-deep in dye, work under the midday sun managing the hides that remain soaked in the vessels. This process of turning animal hides into quality leather products has hardly changed since medieval times. Fez's oldest tannery has been in existence for nearly a thousand years.

INTO THE RED CITY

On the way to Marrakesh is a stop in Ifrane, a mountain resort built by the French in 1928. The first permanent settlement here dates to the 16th century, and the French later used it as a colonial retreat, where it became known as Little Switzerland. Due to its elevation, the town experiences snow during the winter and maintains a cool climate in the summer. Ifrane is also the place where the lowest temperature was ever recorded in Africa: "11 °F ("24 °C) on February 11, 1935. Its quiet streets make for a notable difference from the hustle and bustle of Fez.

While it is not a long drive, it is a winding one through the Middle Atlas Mountains, and I am thankful that I have never suffered from motion sickness. Well once, in the back of a wide car with soft suspension up a winding mountain road, but I don't count that. As the day continues, I pass more time during the drive taking more bus photos.

After getting settled into the hotel, I take a few photos from my balcony. In the morning, I stretch my legs by walking a few blocks around the hotel. I notice that there are many more Europeans in Marrakesh than I found in Fez, and the streets, though just as full of traffic, are certainly wider. The city also has a more Westernized feel than the more traditional Fez. The city was founded in 1070 as the imperial capital of the Almoravid Empire. The city's red walls along various buildings constructed in red sandstone have given the city the nickname of the "Red City." Marrakesh grew rapidly and established itself as a cultural, religious, and trading center for sub-Saharan Africa.

HAREMS AND CAMELS

After my morning stroll is a visit to the Bahia Palace, built in the 19th century. It was once home to a harem and intended to be the greatest palace of its time. It is now home to an impressive display of painted wood, ceramics, and symmetrical gardens. The palace is one of Morocco's most visited tourist attractions, visited more than any other heritage site in the country. We get there early to beat the crowds, though a tour bus arrives just as we depart.

A walk around the Koutoubia Mosque and its surrounding gardens is followed by a trip to the medina and its Djemaa el Fna, Marrakesh's main square, filled with snake charmers and lavishly dressed water sellers. Here I am led into a back room where I haggle for a scarf for a friend back home. It turns out to be a more intense process than expected. I then carefully proceed to take some photos, trying to steer clear of the snake handlers that like to drape a snake around tourist's necks and then charge for photos. I'm neither a fan of snakes nor having my picture taken, so it's best to avoid the whole situation.

Next, a drive through the Gorge of Oued Orika along the banks of the River Orika through the mountains takes some of us to a Berber village and into a Berber home, where we are served mint tea and bread with honey. While the tea is on the verge of being unbearably sweet, we're told it has less sugar than the locals like. It must be a great country to be a dentist. The home's layout is reminiscent of the Tibetan home I visited a few years ago, with living quarters and livestock sharing a tight communal space. I know such encounters are designed for tourists, but I still find it a way to see village life and provide a little to local communities.

THE START OF SOMETHING BEAUTIFUL

Due to my mom's love of films from the 40s and 50s, I grew up very knowledgeable about all things film noir. Some of my favorite actors come from this era: Joseph Cotton, Gene Tierney, and, of course, Humphrey Bogart. Naturally, one cannot think of Bogey without thinking of *Casablanca*. Not surprisingly, the city of the film (which was mostly shot on a sound stage in Hollywood) has nothing to do with the actual city. In reality, Casablanca is Morocco's largest city with well over three million inhabitants. It should also be noted that there are about a dozen Rick's Cafés for tourists to spot and photograph.

Casablanca's Hassan II Mosque is the largest in Morocco and the third largest in the world. It has room for 25,000 worshippers, and a further 80,000 can be accommodated on its adjoining grounds. Its minaret is the world's tallest at 689 feet (210 meters) and is topped with a laser, the light from which is pointed toward Mecca. As the mosque stands on a promontory looking out to the Atlantic Ocean, I use this position to take a couple of coastal shots of the town.

Downtown itself is distinctly post-colonial, with European-style sidewalk cafés and French-inspired bakeries residing in the shadow of half-built high-rises. There is little to differentiate Casablanca's half-finished neighborhoods and animated boulevards from other cities in the developing world, which is probably why it is often glossed over in guidebooks pitching the more glamorous Marrakech or history-rich Fez. I find it has a lot in common with the oldest parts of downtown Los Angeles—a sprawl of cement, people, and cars, none too bothered about tourists.

NORTH TO SOUTH

Rabat, the capital of Morocco, is located on the Atlantic Ocean at the mouth of the river Bou Regreg. It is home to the Royal Palace, one of the only locations in Morocco where one can legally photograph someone wearing a uniform. It is also home to Hassan Tower, begun in 1195 and intended to be the largest minaret in the world. In 1199, sultan Yacoub al-Mansour died, and construction on the mosque and minaret stopped. Interestingly, instead of stairs, the tower is ascended by ramps, allowing the muezzin to ride a horse to the top to issue the call to prayer.

In the morning, it's a 4:30 a.m. wake-up call to drive to Tangier and catch the morning ferry to Tarifa, Spain. I snap a few photos from the ferry's small and windy viewing area as we make the hour-long crossing. After the border check, we start our northern accent to Granada. It's already been a long day, and hunger begins to gnaw at many of us, but our guide seems determined to stop in Torremolinos for lunch. I'm sure he has a regular stop that either offers him a free meal or a cut of the sales, which doesn't help my gurgling stomach.

In the evening we arrive in Granada, an ancient city with historic architecture. Granada is most known for a single monument, the grand Alhambra, which we will be visiting in the morning. However, Granada also boasts a Moroccan souk, a massive cathedral, and flamenco music. While situated among the Sierra Nevada Mountains, the town is very walkable despite its many hills. Soon, the leggy blonde and I head out and get lost. We come across a protest during this outing, along with a half-naked woman in a shop and two lesbians making out in front of another shop. Good times.

THE RED FORTRESS

The Alhambra is a palace and fortress complex of the Moorish rulers of Granada originally completed near the end of the 14th century. While predominantly consisting of Islamic architecture, today it can be seen together with 16th century and later Christian architectural interventions in its many buildings and gardens. Here I take an assortment of photos, paying particular attention to its intricate architectural details. Its hilltop location offers some lovely views of the surrounding area, and its gardens are sprawling.

It also serves as a remnant of the Nasrid Dynasty, the last Islamic kingdom in Western Europe. During its prime, the Alhambra had three main sections: The Alcazaba, a military base housing guards and their families; the palatial zone, containing several palaces for the sultan and his relatives; and the medina, a quarter where court officials lived and worked. There is a reason this is the main attraction in Granada.

The evening finds us back in Madrid. A few of us head out for a last dinner together, then it's off to the market for some provisions for the following day's flights. In the morning, it's a 5:00 a.m. wake-up call to catch my 6:10 a.m. shuttle to the airport. At 6:00 a.m., I give the leggy blonde a promised wake-up knock so that she can catch her morning flight to Estonia, where she'll meet up with her fiancé. I, on the other hand, will return to my solitary life in California. Thankfully, it's only a few weeks before I head off on my next trip.

Jul. 2009 – *Central Europe*

My college offers two summer sessions, one in June and one in July, and I had gotten into the habit of teaching one while traveling during the other. This summer, I decided to focus on traveling and followed my Spain, Portugal, and Morocco trip with a tour of Central Europe. It was advertised as the "Best of Eastern Europe," but my guide was adamant that it was Central, not Eastern Europe, that we would be exploring. This trip surveyed five countries— Austria, the Czech Republic, Poland, Slovakia, and Hungary— mainly using public transport. I figured such a trip would give me a taste of each country, and I could return to each for a more in-depth experience, which I have done in subsequent years.

THE GOLDEN APPLE

Vienna is a beautiful city, once deemed the city of the "golden apple" by the Ottomans. It seems there is something striking on every block, mixed with the mundane found in any big city. The main roads are filled with tram tracks and the skies with tram lines. We set off on a morning walking tour, first exploring the area near our hotel. We then proceed downtown, which includes the Romanesque and Gothic St. Stephen's Cathedral. This is a city on a grand scale, with some of its buildings spanning entire blocks.

After the tour, I set out with one of my group into the Jewish district. There is always a sadness visiting such areas, knowing the damage of World War II and the hatred it bestowed. We then head over to KunstHausWien, a former factory building redesigned and transformed by Friedensreich Hundertwasser into a repository for his art. The site features such irregular elements as uneven floors and misshapen windows, along with amalgamations of metal, glass, brick, and ceramic tile.

We then make a mad metro dash back to the hotel area as I try to get to a store before they close at six. I'd seen a beautiful music box in their window while exploring the area the night before. I sprint from the metro station to the block it is on. The store is within sight at 5:57 p.m., so I make a run for it. After a bit of confusion about which music box I'm interested in and a rejected credit card, I find I have enough Euros on me to buy my Austrian souvenir. Now to pack it safely for the rest of the trip. And find an ATM to cover the Euros I just spent.

ENTERING BOHEMIA

In the morning, we catch a local train to Cesky Krumlov, a small city in the South Bohemian Region of the Czech Republic, best known for its architecture and the art of its historic old town. Construction of the town and its castle began in the late 13th century at a ford in the Vltava River, which snakes through the region. In fact, Krumlov can be translated as "crooked meadow," referring to a bend of the Vltava. The town's name begins with Cesky ("Bohemian") to distinguish it from Moravsky Krumlov, which can be found in south Moravia.

After dropping my bag at the hotel (and hitting my head the first of many times on the low stairwell), I start to explore the town. Along with its striking castle, Cesky Krumlov features an old town square with Renaissance and Baroque architecture. As you can walk from one side of town to the other in 20 minutes, I take my time and try to take in every feature and nuance. I find that I'm starting to get a little obsessed with the castle tower, though this does not deter me from taking many more photos of it.

After dinner, some of us head out for drinks, including a sampling of some local beers and spirits. As time goes on, it just ends up being myself, our tour leader, and my roommate. Note to self: Never try to compete with a Slovak (guide) or an Aussie (roommate) when it comes to alcohol—you will not win. By the end of the night, I'm sitting beside a girl named Zen, who takes some drunken photos of us with my camera. I return the favor by taking some tipsy photos of her with her camera before calling it a night.

WHAT HANGOVER?

The shower in my room requires that someone tall like myself shower at an angle, which is an added challenge after my late night. Once (primarily) soap-free, I fight off a bit of nausea and a slight fever in order to explore more of the city. There is a southern area I have not yet seen that I head off toward. As I explore, I learn that the map I picked up at the hotel has no sense of scale, though its twists and turns seem good approximations. Nothing is too far away in this town, so I'm not too concerned with unexpectedly long distances.

Though I should probably go back to my room and get in a nap as my head is starting to pound, I decide instead to hike up to the Chapel on the Mountain of the Cross. As my map is not to scale, I find myself wandering into a neighborhood before realizing I've missed a turn that appeared to be further along on the map. I have been told that there is an excellent view of the city from the chapel. While this turns out to be accurate, it is the chapel that I find most picturesque. I also become enamored with the markers along the trail used to indicate the stations of the cross during pilgrimages and look to photograph each one, ticking off the number of stations in my mind as I proceed.

I call it an early evening after dinner. My roommate and guide have another late night drinking, and sometime in the early hours, my roommate returns. We are sharing a rather large room with many beds situated at the top of the hotel, which accounts for the angles to be found in the shower and throughout the room. I can then hear him tripping over beds and feeling along the angled walls as he tries to find the door to the bathroom in the dark.

JOSEF K. WAS HERE

In the morning, we drive into Prague. This city has interested me ever since my existential college years spent reading Kafka, among many others. Thoughts of *The Trial* and *The Castle* fill my imagination during the ride. Not only do Kafka and I share a birthday (July 3), but now I will be in his city.

Exploration of the city brings me to Saint Vitus' Cathedral, located entirely within Prague Castle and containing the tombs of many Bohemian kings. It is an arresting example of Gothic architecture and is the country's largest and most important church. Construction of the present-day cathedral began in 1344 upon the site of an earlier 10th-century rotunda and, in all, took nearly six centuries to complete.

After the cathedral, I explore the city a bit on foot before dinner. Still not feeling well (persistent cough and sore throat), I call it an early night again and try to get some rest. I also have some wash-and-wear laundry to do. My roommate in Peru turned me on to wash-and-wear, including underwear and socks, and I haven't looked back since switching.

In the morning, it's back on a tram and into another part of town. We stop for coffee in a café designed in the cubist architectural style, then explore a bit more of the city. Initially, I sit at an eatery lining the town square for lunch, then I see the prices and remember why this is never a good idea. I discretely vacate my seat and opt for a small restaurant several narrow blocks from the square where I have a very good meal. Afterward, I put the city map in my pocket and see what I can find.

THE LOVELY PIANIST

My map-free wanderings eventually find me back at the tram stop where we had gotten off in the morning, so I decide to follow the tracks for a bit. As I am often standing on tram rides and unable to look through the windows, this gives me a chance to see what I have been driving past. I eventually come across the New Town Hall Tower, which I ascend, taking a few photos along the way. As the steps become steeper and narrower and the light diminishes, I am reminded of Hitchcock's *Vertigo*. I used to suffer from some vertigo myself, but in Mexico, hiking along the edges of Cooper Canyon, I realized that it seemed to have dissipated. Once reaching the top, most of the viewing area is encased in wire, so I try to take some creative shots including the wire. Periodically there is a small opening without wire, so I take some wireless photos as well.

I snap a few last photos on my way back to the hotel, where I freshen up before dinner. It turns out that the receptionist is a friend of our tour guide, and she joins us for dinner and a night walk of the area. Prague is a stunning city at night. As we continue to wander about, members of our group call it a night. Eventually, the night finds the receptionist, me, our guide, and my roommate in a bar for a few drinks. When not working 12+ hours at the hotel, she tells me she is a music teacher and pianist. As I was classically trained on guitar myself, we compare notes on favorite composers and musical styles. Knowing I will never keep up with my guide or roommate, I sip my drinks as the night goes on. This is not helping my cough or sore throat, but evenings like this don't often come along when traveling, and I want to make the most of it.

DEM BONES

In the 14th century, Kutna Hora rivaled Prague as Bohemia's most important town. This was due to the silver ore that ran through the rocks beneath it. Then, as tends to happen, the silver ran out. Today, it is probably most known for the Sedlec Ossuary, a small Roman Catholic chapel located beneath the Cemetery Church of All Saints. The ossuary contains approximately 40,000 to 70,000 human skeletons, which have been artistically arranged to form decorations and furnishings for the chapel.

Kutna Hora is also home to St. Barbara's Church, whose construction was begun in 1388 but, due to many interruptions, not completed until 1905. Gothic in design, it was initially intended to be probably twice its current size. Given the 500+ years it took to achieve what there is, I can see why they didn't go with the original design. While its exterior is striking, it is its interior that I find most photogenic, including elaborate stained-glass windows and a high, vaulted ceiling. Medieval frescoes depicting the daily life of the mining town along with religious themes have been partially preserved.

I explore the city a bit more before heading on a mining tour. I'm given a white cloth coat (offering visibility, not protection), a hard hat, and a war surplus light that cannot be angled more than 90 degrees without battery acid spilling out. The group I've joined is warned that the shaft gets low and narrow at points. So, I decide to head in first, figuring that I'll have the rest of the group behind me to push if I get stuck.

TEPLICE NAD METUJI

A series of train rides take us from Prague to Teplice nad Metuji, a small town in the Hradec Kralove region of the Czech Republic. It has around 1800 inhabitants. It is small and quiet, though the staff at the pension we're spending the night at could use some added training. Those hoping to share a meal during lunch find that there is a one-plate, one-fork policy at work here, which is the least of the service problems. When our guide speaks with the owner, he's told we're welcome to stay at the only other accommodations in town if we don't like how he runs things. Good to know the customer isn't always right in Teplice nad Metuji.

After lunch, we begin a hike among the unique sandstone formations that are found throughout the area. A sandy trail takes us through the pines and into the beginning of the rock formations. The site was a regional destination during the 19th and early 20th centuries, as shown by the various languages of stone inscriptions to be found. Near the trail's end are 300 steps leading up to Strmen, a rock tower once occupied by an outlaw's timber castle. While the stairs start out metal, they become wooden and steep near the top. They also narrow considerably. Before reaching the pinnacle, I step aside while waiting for a group of five drunken Germans to make their way down. Once at the top, I take in the view, trying not to think about the 300 steps down.

In the evening, we're all on our best behavior back at the pension. I'm reminded of when my father and I stopped for lunch in a small, rural California town and were stared at by everyone when entering and while seated. When our meal finally did arrive, it was gently tossed on the table, and we were never checked on again.

REMEMBRANCE

Auschwitz-Birkenau was the largest of Nazi Germany's concentration camps, established in Nazi German-occupied Poland, beginning operations in May 1940. In all, it consists of three camps: Auschwitz I, Birkenau (Auschwitz II), and Monowitz (Auschwitz III). It has been approximated that 1.1 million people lost their lives here, about 90% of whom were Jews from almost every country in Europe. Most victims were killed in Auschwitz II's gas chambers. Other deaths were caused by systematic starvation, forced labor, lack of disease control, individual executions, and medical experiments.

Auschwitz I was the original camp, and it served as the administrative center for the whole complex. The camp was initially used for interning Polish intellectuals and resistance movement members and Soviet prisoners of war. At its peak, it held 20,000 prisoners. Our guide is informative and helps guide us through a difficult setting. It is a lot to take in, though I do have to step out of the room containing the children's belongings. To hate a people so much to kill their children is a darkness I will never fathom.

Auschwitz II (Birkenau) was constructed to ease congestion at the main camp. The camp was staffed partly by prisoners, some of whom were selected to be *kapos* (orderlies) and *sonderkommandos* (workers at the crematoria). While most of the structures here no longer stand, there are some barracks kept to the standards of the time. A slightly elevated view reveals the foundations of the barracks that no longer stand used to house the 100,000 prisoner capacity of the site. It is cut in two by train tracks that would bring their one-way journeys to an end.

A PLEASANT SURPRISE

I must admit to not being sure what to expect of Poland. Most of my knowledge of the modern-day country comes from films, notably Krzysztof Kieslowski's *Decalogue* series, which was set in Warsaw. In the series, the city came across as very grey—sky, buildings, people. Krakow, to my surprise, is a charming city featuring Europe's largest medieval town square. It was also named a European Capital of Culture in 2000.

Unlike Prague, which requires mass transit to reach its far corners, Krakow is very accessible by foot. We begin by heading to Old Town, which I photograph in color and black & white. Here can be found the 14th-century St. Mary's Church, one of the best examples of Polish Gothic architecture. 24 hours a day, 365 days a year, a trumpet signals on the hour, played from the top of the taller of Saint Mary's two towers. Then there is the 15th-century Town Hall Tower, the only remaining part of the old Krakow Town Hall, which was demolished in 1820 as part of a plan to open up the Main Square.

Next up is Wawel Hill, which is crowned with a castle and cathedral. The castle, one of Poland's largest, exemplifies nearly all European architectural styles—medieval, renaissance, and baroque period elements can be found there. Finally, a dip into Kazimierz, the Jewish quarter. Founded by King Kazimierz the Great in 1335, it was originally an independent town. In the 15th century, Jews were expelled from Krakow and forced to resettle here. Here we have lunch, and I head back to the hotel to clean up before my deluxe Communist tour of Nowa Huta.

WORKERS' PARADISE

My Central Europe guidebook makes note of a local company offering "entertaining tours of the city's communist-era suburbs, in restored East German cars." As it turns out, three in my group are also interested, so we book a group tour. One of them, a young Chinese man, doesn't understand why the rest of us find the notion of a "deluxe" Communist tour amusing. The tour is usually held in a two-stroke Trabant 601, though, since we all won't fit in this small car, we are taken on tour instead in a Polski Fiat 125. Nothing like the merging of Italian design with Communist manufacturing.

The tour takes us to Nowa Huta, known as "Stalin's gift to Krakow," which was intended to be a model of communist ideology and a workers' paradise. During the tour, we stop at a milk bar, invented to offer cheap home-cooked meals to people working in companies that had no official canteen. Here I have one of the best bean soups I have ever eaten. Good to know communism got some things right.

We also stop by an apartment owned by the tour company, which has not been changed since the 1970s. Here we have a shot of vodka with a pickle chaser and watch a 12-minute propaganda film about Nowa Huta made in 1951. While watching the movie, I wonder why the vodka is served with a pickle chaser until I try it. As the shot burns everywhere it can on the way down my esophagus, I quickly grab the pickle for some relief. Our last stop of the day is Arka Pana (Lord's Ark) Church, built after demand from locals become too great to ignore. After years of delay, it was constructed on the outskirts of Nowa Huta by volunteers from 1967 to 1977.

UNEVEN SURFACES

Tatranska Lomnica is located in the Slovakian part of the High Tatras mountains and will be our home base for the next two nights. It is a skiing and hiking resort best known for its cable car to Lomnicky stit (Lomnica Peak), one of the steepest peaks in Europe. Its summit is 8642 feet (2634 meters) above sea level, making it the second-highest peak in the High Tatras. A local shoemaker claimed he ascended the peak between 1760–1790, though the first recorded climb was made by the English traveler Robert Townson in 1793.

In the morning, we head out for a mountain hike. The cable car leads us up to our starting point, and we head out from there. This would not be a problematic trail except that it is covered in jagged and uneven rocks. When not watching my footing, I occasionally stop to get a glimpse of the view. As our local guide appears as if she could climb all day and night, I try not to dally too long. We break for lunch, where I order a salad, which turns out to be a collection of side dishes on a single plate. After lunch, we come across a series of waterfalls and streams, then take the tram down to a train that takes us back to town.

During the hike, I discover that, while the shoes I travel with have been sufficient for all my previous travels, they did not do so well on this rocky climb. While I try to travel light, my aching (and soon to be blistered) feet wish I had packed my hiking boots. I'm sure this also contributed to my nearly not being able to get out of bed for dinner. I'd decided to rest my legs in the afternoon but both cramped and locked up while trying to make it out of bed. And I was right about our guide— after taking us on our morning and afternoon hike, she was off with her boyfriend for another ascent after leaving us.

OLD AND NEW

A series of trains and buses get us from Tatranska Lomnica to Bratislava, the capital of the Slovak Republic and the country's largest city. Bratislava is in southwestern Slovakia on both banks of the Danube River, and it borders Austria and Hungary, making it is the only national capital that borders two sovereign states. Bratislava and Vienna are also two of Europe's closest national capitals, less than 37 miles (60 km) apart.

We set out for another foot tour of the city, where I take my usual assortment of color and black & white shots. Bratislava is a mixture of old and new. One can find cobblestone roads, pedestrian plazas, 18th-century rococo buildings, sidewalk cafés beside casinos, and a prominent TV tower with an observation deck and rotating restaurant. During our walk, we come across the Church of St. Elisabeth, known as the Blue Church because of the color of its façade, mosaics, and blue-glazed roof. The church doesn't resemble many of the other buildings in Bratislava. It was built during the early 20th century and crafted in Hungarian jugendstil, an artistic movement that was influential primarily in Germany—essentially the German counterpart of Art Nouveau.

After dinner, we set out for a night stroll leading to some impromptu wine tasting at the base of Bratislava Castle. The immense rectangular building has four corner towers and stands on an isolated rocky hill of the Little Carpathians directly above the Danube River. As it is in the middle of Bratislava, it has been a dominant feature of the city for centuries. While the base of the castle is usually a quiet spot, tonight it is filled with drunk teenagers eager to try out their English.

WHO NEEDS SLEEP?

Our last full day is spent in Budapest. Many of my group are staying on for a few more days, but I am flying out the following morning. I plan to return here when I come back to visit the Balkans someday. My mother's family came from Romania via Russia to finally end up in England before my grandfather met my grandmother and brought her and later her family to the States, so I am very interested in exploring this part of Europe. For now, I'll get in all that I can in the time that I have.

We begin our tour with a stop by the Parliament Building, one of Europe's oldest legislative buildings. We then explore the surrounding area on the Pest side of the Danube, which splits the city in two. We then cross the Szechenyi Chain Bridge that takes us to the Buda side of the city. From here, we climb up to a good lookout over the city and then head toward the castle area.

A group of us goes out for drinks after dinner to a club good for people watching, and then a night bus brings us back to our hotel. As I'm catching a very early taxi to the airport, I decide to stay up. When I arrive at the airport, I discover the counter for my airline doesn't open for another hour, so I plop down on the ground with everyone else waiting for their counters to open.

Five countries visited in all during this trip and where do I get my only passport stamp? Frankfurt, where I have a two-hour layover. I did have a momentary freight there as, after handing my passport and boarding card to the agent behind the counter, he looks at me as he says, "Don't worry" while tearing my boarding pass in two. It turns out this was because he was printing me new boarding passes, but for a split second, I wasn't sure what to think.

Dec. 2009 – *Tunisia*

I had planned a trip this winter around Southeast Asia that perfectly fit my college's winter break. However, the day I was supposed to leave, one of my closest friends was getting married, so I had to go back to the drawing board. Somehow, none of the other trips I had considered before choosing Southeast Asia now spoke to me, so I expanded my map. As my last few trips had been multi-country, I figured it would be a nice change to only visit one country this time around. With this thought in mind, I noticed that the company I used for my June trip to Spain, Portugal, and Morocco was now offering a trip to Tunisia, and I knew I'd found my answer. Tunisia is a country I've wanted to visit for a long time. It has been the location of many favorite films, ranging from Star Wars *and* Life of Brian *in the seventies to* The English Patient *in the nineties. I contemplated a bicycle tour there when I was younger, but I never got around to it. Now that I'm a more experienced traveler, it seemed like a good time to finally visit this North African country sandwiched between Algeria and Libya.*

LOST IN TRANSIT (DAY ONE)

I usually fly out of Los Angeles as that often requires at most one layover. Still, as this trip would require two layovers, I chose to fly from Ontario, less than a thirty-minute drive from home. So, for this trip I'm flying from Ontario to Salt Lake City, then on to Paris and finally Tunis. While waiting for my delayed Salt Lake City flight, I received a text from Air France letting me know my Tunis flight had been canceled and thanking me for my understanding.

After nearly an hour on hold, I reached someone at Air France who confirmed that my Tunis flight had been canceled, but they could get me on the last flight out that day. Just as this is being completed, they realize that I'd have to contact Delta since I initially booked with them. When I do, they do not show that my Tunis flight has been canceled, so I head to Paris with the status of my Tunis flight unknown.

As my connection to Paris is now under fifteen minutes, another passenger and I are moved to the very front of the plane to have the best chance of making the next flight. Once in Salt Lake City, we make a mad dash for our Paris connection. We just make it, then sit on the tarmac for over an hour because the plane is overweight. At one point, they are offering $800 to passengers willing to spend the night in Salt Lake City.

We arrive in Paris nearly two hours late and head to a long line for Air France. When it's finally my turn, I am informed that my flight was indeed canceled, but they can get me on a flight leaving the next day and getting me to Tunis by 3 p.m. As the group I am joining is leaving that morning, I suggest just returning me to California.

LOST IN TRANSIT (DAY TWO)

A place for me is found on the 9 p.m. flight, so now it's many hours to kill in the over-priced Paris airport. I had brought along 5 Euros (about 7 dollars), which buys me a very small coffee. In an electronics store, I notice a camera that back home is $450; here it is 450 Euros. My running companion from Salt Lake City also has a delayed departure to Istanbul, so we spend our unintended layover together. As it turns out, we live about twenty minutes from each other and are both teachers. And now, we will always have this Paris layover in common.

My 9 p.m. flight finally leaves at 11 p.m., landing in Tunis just before 2 a.m. A lesser (or perhaps smarter) man would have given up by now, but I soldier on. By 3 a.m., it's clear that my luggage did not make it, so it's off to a long line at lost luggage. I had fully intended on traveling with only carry-ons this trip but changed my mind at the last minute. Now I'm stuck with a day pack that essentially carries only my camera, guidebook, and iPod. Note to self: From now on, include a full set of wash-and-wear clothes in your day back along with all your chargers.

While in the lost luggage queue, every so often, a batch of luggage arrives that may or may not include mine. The decision must then be made to either assume it is not there and stay in line or leave the line hoping it is there and I can catch a cab to my hotel. Of course, if it is not, it's back to the end of the line. I risk it twice to no avail and finally get to report my luggage lost much later than if I had stayed in the queue. The official speaks no English, so it's back to my limited high school French to get my claim in and finally head off to the hotel.

TRAVELING LIGHT

I arrive at my hotel at 4:30 a.m. to discover I have a 6:30 a.m. wake-up call scheduled. I shower and clean my clothes as best I can. I try to rest a bit but am awoken at 6:00 a.m. by the day's first call to prayer from a nearby minaret. Being too tired to be hungry, I skip breakfast and rest in my room till it's time to hop on the bus and head off. I meet our guide and she informs me that should my luggage be found, I will need to retrieve it from the airport, so I will be traveling light a while as we're not back in Tunis for nearly a week.

I meet my traveling companions on the bus as we head to Sousse, known as the "Pearl of the Sahel." It is an important port and commercial center dating back to the Phoenician settlement of Hadrumetum. Here we stop at a marketplace and tour a small mosque. I'm on the lookout for toiletries and socks and, for the first time in my life, wish there were a Wal-Mart around. Instead, I step into a shop looking for some shirts and soon find myself haggling for some silver jewelry. I only want one piece but end up with four. Guess my bartering skills still need to be honed.

Next is a stop in Monastir, where we visit Habib Bourguiba's family mausoleum. Bourguiba was a Tunisian statesman and the first president of the Republic of Tunisia from July 25, 1957, until November 7, 1987. The mausoleum began construction in 1963 and was only opened to the public after Bourguiba's passing in 2000. Bourguiba's many government reforms included female emancipation, public education, a campaign to improve literacy, and building the country's infrastructure. In addition to the former president and his first wife, the mausoleum also houses the bodies of his parents, his siblings, and other members of his family.

EL JEM (A.K.A. THYSDRUS)

The afternoon finds us in El Jem, famous for its amphitheater capable of seating 35,000 spectators. Only Rome's Colosseum (about 45,000 spectators) and the ruined theater of Capua (60,000 spectators) are larger. The city was known to the Romans as Thysdrus. In a less arid climate than found today, Thysdrus prospered as a notable center of olive oil production and export. By the early 3rd century, when the amphitheater was built, Thysdrus rivaled Hadrumetum (now Sousse) as the second city of Roman North Africa after Carthage.

The amphitheater, thought to be mainly used for gladiator shows and chariot races, is quite impressive. It is one of the best-preserved Roman stone ruins in the world and is unique in all of Africa. I explore its interior, climb to its top, then wander about its underside. There are so many angles to be found; I could be left here to photograph all day. I finally pull myself away, exploring a bit of the town around the ruins. I take a few creative shots, including a silhouetted self-portrait. I have never been one for having my photo taken, let alone self-portraits, so this will have to do. Before leaving, I get in a few more exterior shots of the amphitheater—I can't help myself.

The evening finds us in Sfax, Tunisia's second-largest city. Nearby our hotel is a market where I'm able to pick up some toiletries and underthings. I also pick up a few t-shirts and a nicer button-down shirt as it will be Christmas in a few days, and I'm assuming a dinner out. I choose colors that go with the only pair of trousers I have, which are thankfully stain-resistant and easy to clean. So now I'm living out of a day pack and two plastic bags. Second note to self: Also include a hat in your day pack from now on.

DIGGING IN THE DIRT

In the morning, we walk about Sfax and find ourselves in its medina. Compared to Fez, this medina is modern, and its layout is straightforward. It represents the best conserved Arab-Muslim town planning in the Mediterranean Basin and its monuments have been classified as national historical monuments since 1912. This is followed by a stop in Gabès, an oasis by the sea known for its spice market. After exploring the market, I wandered about the market's outskirts some, becoming intrigued by a series of carved, wooden doors.

Next is Matmâta, where some local Berber residents live in traditional underground "troglodyte" structures. These structures are created by digging a large pit in the ground. Around the perimeter of this pit, artificial caves are then dug to be used as rooms, with some homes comprising multiple pits connected by trench-like passageways. This type of home served as the location of the Lars Homestead, home to Luke Skywalker, in the *Star Wars* movies.

Interestingly, it was not generally known until 1969 that there were regular settlements in this area besides wandering nomadic tribes. That year, severe rains flooded the troglodyte homes and caused many of them to collapse. A delegation was sent to Gabès in order to get help from the authorities. The visit came as a surprise, but assistance was provided, and the above-ground settlement of Matmâta was built. However, most of the people continued their lives in re-built underground homes, and only a few of the families moved to the new surface dwellings.

Soon after, we arrive in Douz, our stop for the night. But before dinner, I have a lovelorn camel waiting for me.

LOVE AND SALT

Before taking a camel ride into the Sahara, our guide makes note that it is mating season. Not to worry, we are told, because all our camels are male. That said, we may notice some strange behavior, including whistling, frothing at the mouth, and the inflation of a gland under the tongue, making a very loud sputtering sound when it moves in and out. My camel, of course, is experiencing every one of these symptoms. He also keeps looking behind him and brushing into other camels. Even so, I'm still able to get in some single-handed photos.

In the morning, we head for Tozeur. Near Kebili, we make a stop to witness some mini mountains formed by sand and wind. Here I come across what appears to be a hawk, though it could be a falcon—where's a birder when you need one? This is followed by a stop along the salt lake of Chott el Jerid, covering nearly 2000 square miles (around 5200 square km). According to legend, it was here that the Greek goddess Athena was born. There is a road running through the salt lake now, making the journey from Douz to Tozeur much more direct.

We are in Tozeur early. After a brief rest, it's off to do some off-roading into the mountain oasis of Chebika. Okay, so it's not really off-roading, more like a long drive in Toyota Land Cruisers, but let's not be pedantic. We stop along the way to walk among a caravan of camels, where I can't resist taking a few creative soil shots. This is followed by a drive into Chebika, very near the Algerian border. We try to get our driver to take us there—we only want a passport stamp—but he understandably resists. Here we are left to explore the remains of this mountain oasis and hike into the hills.

ENGLISH MAP, ARABIC SIGNS

This is followed by a visit to Tamerza, the largest mountain oasis in Tunisia. It has a canyon and an old town, which was abandoned after the river flooded for 22 days in 1969 (the same flooding that brought about awareness of the underground inhabitants of Matmâta). The town is located north of the salt lakes and receives fresh water from the nearby hills. It is well-known for its clear water cascades and springs that irrigate its park. Here we explore the waterfalls while ignoring the ever-present salesmen. I notice a way onto the top of the falls, so I wander over. Tunisians refer to the falls as "the hanging balcony overlooking the Sahara Desert," and I can see why. The last stop of the day is Midès with its abandoned village. I'm assuming the 1969 floods caused its evacuation as well.

Later, a group of us heads into town looking to have dinner at a restaurant I've spotted in my guidebook. Unfortunately, while my map is in English, all of the road signs are in Arabic, so we inevitably get lost. I'm leading a group of five women, one of which caught my eye our first morning on the bus, and I've been trying to speak with her whenever I get the chance. Not sure I'm making the best impression here, as even my broken French doesn't seem to be helping. While stopping to ask for directions a few times, we finally find ourselves on a main road and locate a place for dinner. It's not the place from my guidebook, but by now the darkness has grown along with our hunger. The menu is in French, but we manage, and I get a camel steak. I can't help thinking back to my lovelorn camel the prior evening and what he would think of me eating one of his cousins.

BLAST FROM THE PAST

In the morning, we head into an oasis near Tozeur. With hundreds of thousands of palm trees, it is a large oasis and exporter of dates. In ancient times, before the arrival of motorized vehicles, the oasis was important for the transport through the Sahara, which took place in caravans. In antiquity, it was an important Roman outpost. Here we are shown a demonstration of how a female date palm is pollinated. This is followed by a visit to the medina, featuring traditional architecture, fashion, and craftsmanship.

In the afternoon, we make a stop at Sbeitla. Nearby are the Roman ruins of Sufetula, containing the best-preserved Forum temples in Tunisia. Some inscriptions found in the city suggest that the settlement had success during the 2nd century, reaching great prosperity through the olive industry. The city began to decline during the Late Empire. At that time, the city was occupied by Vandals, a fact that is demonstrated by the appearance of temples dedicated to the barbarian gods.

It's Christmas Eve, and our hotel has planned a special nine-course, nearly four-hour-long dinner for us. There is also a duo mainly playing love songs from the eighties, along with the occasional Elvis impersonation. It's like the prom I never went to. I'm tempted to break into a rendition of "Hava Nagila" just to stir things up, but I resist. It is my great good fortune to be having dinner beside the most beautiful woman on my tour, who in my eyes is also the most beautiful woman in Tunisia, so I behave. She is surprised when the guy who's been living out of a daypack and two plastic bags comes to dinner in a pressed shirt.

A CHRISTMAS MIRACLE

It's Christmas morning, and we're heading to the ruins of Dougga. Before, it's a visit to Kairouan's Great Mosque. Seven pilgrimages to this mosque are considered the equivalent of one pilgrimage to Mecca. As such, Kairouan is regarded as a holy place for Muslims. In addition, due to its age and architectural features, the minaret of the Great Mosque of Kairouan has served as the prototype for all the minarets of the western Islamic world, both in North Africa and in Andalusia.

According to UNESCO, which qualified Dougga as a World Heritage Site in 1997, the location represents "the best-preserved Roman small town in North Africa." It is simply a fantastic site rich with Punic, Numidian, ancient Roman, and Byzantine history. And I am here on Christmas day with the most beautiful woman in Tunisia by my side. Thank you, Santa. As we explored the site together, she has me help her take a photo similar to one she saw on a postcard while we were entering the site.

Upon our arrival back in Tunis, I make a run to the airport to retrieve my lost bag. I'm told there is a large room full of unclaimed bags I will have to sort through. I have visions of the end of *Raiders of the Lost Ark* when the Ark of the Covenant is being placed into storage. The reality is not quite so expansive. The bags are sorted by airline, though mine is not among the lost bags of Air France. Out of the corner of my eye, I catch the back of my bag, and we are finally reunited. Now that I have an entire bag of clothes, I decide I'm going to change at least for dinner the next few nights to make up for my improvised wardrobe thus far.

SCENTS AND SACRIFICES

My new companion and I walk down to Tunis' medina in the morning, which contains over 700 monuments, including palaces, mosques, mausoleums, madrasas, and fountains dating from the 12th century. Once we've reached one of the mosques, a local approaches us and invites us to a location where there is a panoramic view of the medina. While we know there will be at least a tip involved, he seems honest, so we follow him to a carpet shop that used to be a royal residence. The roof does provide an excellent view of the surrounding area.

Our impromptu guide then invites us back to his shop—he sells perfumes and scented oils—and we both buy a small bottle. As we leave, we're unsure how to proceed once we're reached the same mosque where we met him, so our new friend returns and invites us to tea. He takes us to an area off the main road with no tourists in sight. We sit while he tells us some of his story. I also snap a photo of my lovely companion with our guide, figuring an email address is now needed to send her the picture.

We make our way back into town, and our group heads into Carthage, which was the capital city of the ancient Carthaginian civilization and one of the most important trading hubs of the ancient Mediterranean. It was also one of the most affluent cities of the classical world. Before visiting the main site, we stop by the Tophet of Carthage, a once sacred place where human sacrifices (primarily children, it is believed) were offered to the gods. The principal gods of Carthage were the sun god Baal and the moon goddess Tanit. The location is believed to have been built on the spot where the legendary foundress of Carthage, Elissa, landed in Tunisia.

CITY BY THE SEA

The city of Carthage is located on the eastern side of Lake Tunis, across from the center of Tunis. According to Roman legend, it was founded in 814 BCE by Phoenician colonists from Tyre under the leadership of Queen Dido (Elissa). It became a large and prosperous city and thus a significant power in the Mediterranean. Not much is left of it today, and its view of the sea is shielded by a wall, though the smell of the sea is in the air. This doesn't stop me from getting in a plethora of color and black & white photos.

After Carthage is a stop in Sidi Bou Said, known for the extensive use of blue and white colors all over the town. The city is named for a religious figure who lived there, Abu Said al-Baji. It has a reputation as a town of artists, as many famous artists have lived here or visited at some point. The most notable include German painter Paul Klee and French writer Andre Gide. There is a quaintness to the town, though it is a tourist draw, as its many shops attest. My new companion and I take a break with some tea in a nearby café.

Our last stop of the day is the Bardo Museum, featuring an extensive collection of Roman mosaics. It is one of the most important museums in the region and is considered the second museum of the African continent after the Egyptian Museum of Cairo in terms of the wealth of its collection. It traces the history of Tunisia over several millennia and across several civilizations through a wide variety of archaeological pieces. This is followed by a return to our hotel, where I have my last dinner with my group and my lovely traveling companion.

THE ADVENTURE CONTINUES

The day starts off well. My flight from Tunis to Paris departs and arrives on time. I make it through security and find my gate. Then the fun begins. Thanks to al-Qa'ida's failed Christmas Day bombing of Northwest Airlines Flight 253, security is high. At the gate, shoes and jackets are removed, and passengers are frisked front and back. Large carry-on bags are checked, and smaller carry-ons are thoroughly searched. Subsequently, we arrive in Atlanta late. After collecting and checking my bag, a display shows my flight for Ontario has not yet left, so I make a mad dash for the gate only to find that I've just missed it. I call the airline's help desk but am told that since the delay was caused by security in Paris, they can't offer me a hotel for the night but do get me on a flight to Ontario in the morning. I walk out to the line of waiting hotel shuttles and pick one I know to be reasonably priced. Fortunately, once there, the receptionist takes pity on me and puts together a toiletry assortment.

In the morning, I'm expecting a direct flight to Ontario (what I had missed the night before) but instead find I am flying to Denver, then Salt Lake City, and finally Ontario. In Denver, I get shaky and realize all I've had to eat the last twelve hours was orange juice for dinner and a large coffee for breakfast, so I find myself a café and resist the temptation to order a Denver omelet. The remaining flights are thankfully uneventful.

In all, I've lost a day and a half to delays and cancellations this trip. Before heading to bed, I do get a quick email off to my travel companion, who must be wondering why she hasn't heard from me in two days.

Mar. 2010 – *Panama*

For some reason, it wasn't until this year that I realized I could sneak a trip in during my Spring Break. I browsed the offerings of some of the tour companies I've used in the past, limiting my search to the Western Hemisphere as I didn't have time for long-haul flights. One company I'd used before was offering a new trip to Panama that perfectly fit my break. As this trip ticked all my boxes, I figured it was a sign I should head down there. I'll admit to not knowing much about Panama, except for the canal and the U.S. invasion in the late 1980s. Unfortunately, this is true of many Central American countries that are often seen as dangerous or drug-infested here in the United States. While some may have their struggles, many of my favorite travels have come from Central America, and Panama was no exception.

THE PERSON YOU SEE WHEN YOU'RE YOUNG

As my fortieth birthday is approaching, I suppose it's not unexpected that I should find myself looking back. When I was younger, my passion was writing. I was not only going to be a writer but a great writer. I wanted to rival William Faulkner, with Cormac McCarthy revealing that excellent writing could still exist in this modern age. While an undergraduate, I drafted out two novels and a short story collection. Stories and poems of mine started appearing in small journals and anthologies. I even received a personal rejection for my first novel from a noted publisher, so I figured I was on the right path.

I shifted to mostly writing poetry in grad school, as poems can be quicker to draft than a story. My first poetry collection was published a decade later, with my second following a few years afterward. I have two other collections in draft form and a third researched but not written. The only thing is, I rarely write these days and can't imagine completing any of these unfinished collections. I've become an academic and a scholar, the demon-driven writer in me driven down. Oh, and there's also the travel and the photo editing that follows every trip.

One writes for self-discovery; one travels to escape. Or maybe it's the other way round. Regardless, I am escaping to Panama this time, one of the last Central American countries I haven't set foot in. So far, I have thoroughly enjoyed every Central American country I have visited and hope Panama will be the same. Besides, the Panama Canal is approaching its hundredth birthday soon; maybe we can commiserate together.

THE FOUR PIRATES

Until recently, the leading tourist trade of Panama was through ports of call, where hordes of cruise ship inhabitants would disembark for a few hours of sightseeing and shopping. As such, Panama's accommodations for the overnight crowd are still developing. For instance, only recently have tour buses become air-conditioned and, while wake-up calls at hotels are enthusiastically written down, they are rarely, if ever, made. Before leaving on this trip, many people asked me what was in Panama. I do not have an answer. Apart from some knowledge of the history of the canal, I am shamefully unaware of this country. That alone is reason enough to visit.

We start our first full day in the country with a visit to Panama Viejo, the remains of the old Panama City. First is a visit to a museum, where my group is greeted by four college girls dressed as pirates, who serve as our guides here and later at the ruins. One even has an eye patch. As most of the placards in the museum are in Spanish, they also serve as translators.

Panama Viejo was founded in 1519 by the conquistador Pedrarías Dávila and is the oldest European settlement on the Pacific coast of the Americas. The remains of the old town are now surrounded by the modern city, which makes for some interesting contrasts. Its most striking feature is its tower, which is available for climbing.

While I explore the area, I take my usual assortment of photos, stopping every so often to wipe the sweat from my brow. To break the effects of the humidity, I order a banana shake at a nearby stand, which is very refreshing. It also leads others to give the stand a try, so I have done my part to spur on the local economy.

MIGHTY BIG LOCKS

Think Panama, and you think of the canal. We will be sailing through it tomorrow, but today is a visit to Miraflores Locks. These are the last two locks of the canal before entering the Pacific Ocean (for ships coming from the Caribbean) or the first two locks of the canal (for ships coming from the Pacific). Miraflores is also the name of the small lake that separates these locks from the Pedro Miguel Locks upstream. In the Miraflores Locks, vessels are lifted (or lowered) 54 feet (16.5 meters) in two stages, allowing them to transit to or from the Pacific Ocean port of Balboa in Panama City. Ships cross below the Bridge of the Americas, connecting North and South America.

Each of the locks drain 26 million gallons of water and lower vessels about 39 inches (one meter) per minute, taking about 8 to 10 minutes to lower the water level 27 feet. Large vessels only have a two-foot clearance on either side and are guided through by trains with wires. It is a slow but fascinating experience to watch. The overall length of the locks, including their approach walls, is around 1.9 miles (3 km). The locks were one of the greatest engineering works to be undertaken when they opened in 1914. No other concrete construction of similar size was undertaken until the Hoover Dam in the 1930s.

After dinner is a folklore show. It's performed in one of the hotel's undecorated conference rooms, which is different. And while I don't take any photos, there is a very intriguing move performed by two of the male dancers involving them doing the splits in order to then bend over to put on hats that have been placed on the floor. Now that's flexibility.

HALF A CANAL

In all, the Panama Canal is about 50 miles (80 km) long and can take between 9 and 12 hours to pass through. Today we are entering at Gamboa, on the southern tip of Gatun Lake. Gamboa was one of a handful of permanent Canal Zone townships built to house employees of the Panama Canal and their families. This is about the halfway point. We are heading toward the Pacific Ocean and will be passing through both the Pedro Miguel and Miraflores Locks—three of the six locks of the canal.

Before reaching the Pedro Miguel Locks, there is the Centennial Bridge, opened in 2004, and only the second permanent crossing over the canal. It was built to complement the congested Bridge of the Americas and to supersede it as the carrier of the Pan-American Highway. Next, we enter the Pedro Miguel Locks, along with two sailboats and a vast ship carrying automobiles. Experiencing the locks firsthand is a remarkable experience as the chamber lowers our ship 29 feet (9 meters) to Lake Miraflores.

Next are the Miraflores locks, which we visited yesterday as observers. Today we are one of the observed. We then come to the Bridge of the Americas, the first permanent crossing over the canal, built between 1959 and 1962 by the United States for $20 million. From its completion until the opening of the Centennial Bridge in 2004, the Bridge of the Americas was a vital part of the Pan-American Highway. We then head into Balboa harbor. Once docked, it's about an hour's drive to Paraiso, our home for the next two days. Paraiso is located just north of the Panama Canal's Pedro Miguel Locks, so we have come full circle.

WHAT WOULD CRISTOBEL THINK?

In the morning, we head north to the Caribbean side of the country, which has a much more tropical feel. Our first stop is Portobelo, founded in 1597. The first thing one sees entering the tiny town is San Felipe de Portobelo Church, home to the Cristo Negro ("Black Christ") statue. The life-size wooden statue of Christ was found on the shores of the town's harbor. One legend says that the figure was carved in Spain. During the 17th century, it was carried in a Colombian vessel to be installed in the New World. Due to a storm, the ship was forced to dock at Portobelo. A sudden storm set in when the ship was scheduled to depart, preventing the ship from setting sail. This repeatedly happened. Accrediting this phenomenon to the statue, the superstitious sailors threw the box containing the statue into the sea. The storm subsided, and the ship moved on.

Beyond this are the ruins of San Jeronimo Fort. Much of this fort was taken down by American engineers, who used its walls to create the breakwater protecting the northern end of the Panama Canal. Explorations of the fortress completed, I wonder about town some, then head to the remains of another fort, Fuerte Santiago. From here, there is a trail leading to Mirador Peru, a lookout above the area.

Our stay in Portobelo finished, we head to Colón, founded by Christopher Columbus (Cristobel Colón in Spanish) in 1502. Initially, we were going to spend two nights here, but safety concerns led to a change of location. Recent reports put Colón's unemployment rate around 40%, with the poverty rate even higher. One can tell that it was once grand, though now derelict and increasingly desperate.

TATTOOS AND DANCING INDIANS

Before returning to Paraiso, we stop by Gatun Lake, where we catch a view of the Gatun Locks and surrounding area. We also see some of the construction of the canal's expansion, due to be completed in 2014. This expansion involves the construction of much larger, more technologically advanced locks. It will double the canal's capacity by adding a new lane of traffic, allowing for more ships, and increasing the width and depth of the lanes and locks to allow larger ships to pass.

Of the several dozen native tribes that inhabited Panama when the Spanish arrived, only seven remain. One of these, the Emberá, inhabits the jungle of the eastern Panama Province and the Darien. They are a riverine people, traditionally building their houses along the banks of rivers. Although most Emberá people live in villages, towns, or urban centers today, many established Emberá communities are still found along riverbanks. Here they live in simple thatched huts and make tightly woven baskets from palm fibers along with handicrafts from tagua nuts and the cocobolo tree.

To reach one of these Emberá villages, we set off across the Chagres River in the morning. Upon our arrival at the village, I snap some photos. The natives then put on a dance for us. At one point, I'm brought on to the dance floor. With any luck, no photos of this exist. Later some of my group receive temporary tattoos painted on by the native women. At the same time, I'm able to catch a nice picture of a native girl coming out of her thatched hut.

SAINTS AND CHICKEN WIRE

The town of El Valle is situated in the crater of an extinct volcano and ringed by verdant forests and jagged peaks. All accounts describe it as picturesque, though I think I may be missing something. Then again, after a ninety-minute drive, we don't stay long enough to get a chance to see what may make the area "picturesque."

We begin our visit with a walk around El Nispero Zoo. It is a modest location filled with potential, much like one's impression of Colón. I divide my time here photographing the surroundings and the animals, ranging from parrots and swans to alligators and monkeys, most behind various forms of chicken wire. Who knew there were so many types of hens? I've never been much for zoos, preferring to see wildlife in its native habitat, but understand that not everyone can go to where the wildlife is.

Next, we head into town, home to one of Panama's largest handicrafts markets. Today is a celebration of the town's saint, so many people are packed into its small church, and there is some extra wear to be found for sale. As we will be having a late lunch today, I look for something to eat while exploring and discover mystery meat on a stick—Anthony Bourdain would be proud. Tastes like chicken.

Upon our return to Play Blanca, I wander the beach looking for some interesting photos. During my exploration, I am stopped by security to verify that I am a guest at the resort. It is unusual for me to be staying at a resort—my typical accommodations tend to be a bit more rustic. Not that I'm complaining, I'm just saying that I wouldn't trust me either.

AND THE LIST GOES ON AND ON

In the morning, we begin our return to Panama City. Along the way, we stop for lunch on the Causeway Islands, four small islands by the Pacific entrance of the Panama Canal. They are linked to the mainland by a causeway made from rock extracted during the excavations from the Panama Canal. In part, the causeway was meant to serve as a breakwater for the entrance. Manuel Noriega built a private house on one of the islands, which was destroyed and looted during his ouster. After lunch, I explore the area and snap some photos, the outline of the city in the background. I also pick up a Panama hat. Rather than the more typical black band, I opt for one with a woven band.

We then head to a Kuna Indian market. Like the Emberá, the Kuna are one of the seven remaining indigenous tribes. As we have a while here, I head down the road to explore Balboa, founded by the United States during the construction of the Panama Canal. The town, like most towns in the Canal Zone, was served by Canal Zone Government operated schools, post office, police and fire stations, commissary, cafeteria, movie theater, service center, bowling alley, and other recreational facilities and company stores. The town was also home to two private banks, several churches, civic clubs (including the Elks Club and the Knights of Columbus), a Masonic Lodge, a YMCA, several historic monuments, and a miniature Statue of Liberty donated by the Boy Scouts of America.

It then begins to rain, so I head back to the market for shelter (and to buy a certain someone a certain something).

OLD TOWN PANAMA

In the morning, a group of us sets off to explore Casco Viejo, the historic center of Panama City. While it is possible to walk there from our hotel, our guide books us taxis, warning us that there is a part of town between the two locations that is still pro-Noriega and anti-America after the U.S. invasion of Panama in late 1989. The invasion resulted in the capture of Noriega after ten days secured in the Holy See's embassy. He was then detained as a prisoner of war and later taken to the United States.

Casco Viejo is a mix of different architectural styles: Caribbean, Spanish, Art Deco, and French Colonial all mix in a site of less than 800 buildings. I begin my excursion by heading toward Plaza de Francia, the southern tip of the region. Here one finds vendors, street musicians, and some restorations. Then I start to head more inland, where repairs are less prevalent. At the Plaza de la Independencia, one finds the Cathedral, which is striking with its white towers. I spend a lot of time exploring this area as there is a fascinating mix of architectural styles in varying degrees of disrepair. There's also an excellent ice cream shop.

In the evening, we head out for our farewell dinner at a restaurant in the Miraflores Locks. As our trip essentially began here, it is a fitting place to end. It also gives us a chance to see the canal at night. It turns out that two in our group work for the travel company and were accompanying us as it is a relatively new offering. In fact, the itinerary had changed since I booked it and was subject to change again. I'm glad I had the itinerary I did as I felt it was a good blend of city, jungle, and beach.

LESSONS LEARNED

So, what have I learned about Panama? I came in with very little knowledge other than what I had learned from the news over the years and from my guidebook, so what am I coming away with?

Geographically, I now know that Panama is the only country with oceans on both its northern and southern borders, thanks to its location and tilde shape. Its second-largest city, Colón, has no stoplights and very few stop signs. The government tried adding stoplights at one point in time, but they only served to confuse the locals.

Panama is situated south of the hurricane track and is generally not affected by these tropical storms (one of the main reasons the canal was constructed here). It has 1000 miles of coast and 1000 islands on the Pacific side, and 800 miles of coast and 600 islands on the Caribbean side. While some areas are still scarred by the U.S. invasion of 1989, and some areas are more tourist-friendly than others. In fact, we were informed by our guide that only recently has air conditioning put into tourist buses, with a few rows of seats removed for comfort.

The country does have some sights that should not be missed. Highlights for me: Colón (never experienced a city quite like it); Portobelo (the forts should not be missed); and, of course, the canal itself. Being here to witness the canal's expansion is a part of history, and I would love to return someday to see its completion.

May 2010 – *Southern Caucasus*

In wanting to keep to my seven continents by age forty plan, this summer was supposed to be a lengthy trip to Australia, New Zealand, and Fiji. However, having met my future wife in Tunisia, I decided it was more important to spend the summer with her and build our relationship. As she had limited vacation time having just returned from visiting me in Southern California, I decided to get in a three-week trip before settling in for the rest of the summer with her in London. This was my first tour where each country saw a different guide and driver. I felt sorry for our Georgian guide as everyone had fallen in love with our Armenian guide, and there was no way she was going to live up, even though she was more than capable. This will also mark my last trip without my future wife. Having met in Tunisia, I will propose to her in London after this trip and she will be my traveling companion from here on.

HIGH ON A PLANE

The South Caucasus is a geographical region on the edge of Eastern Europe and Western Asia, straddling the southern Caucasus Mountains. It is comprised of the countries of Armenia, Georgia, and Azerbaijan and is a region of betweens. Besides setting between Asia and Europe, it is also located between the Black and Caspian seas, Russia and the Middle East, Christianity and Islam. As I am interested in Eastern Europe and Asia in general, this seemed like a unique area to explore as it is where East meets West.

I'm flying to London this trip, where I have a lengthy layover that I'll be spending with my girlfriend, whom I haven't seen since early April. On the way there, I decide to take a sleeping pill as I never sleep on planes and would like to be somewhat coherent for our time together. About halfway through the ten-hour flight, I awaken quite nauseous and, on my way to the rear restroom, get light-headed. Someone seated asks, "Are you okay?" just before I find myself collapsed in the aisle. Crew rush to help me up, which leads to me being given oxygen and strapped into one of the flight attendant's seats at the rear of the plane, where I'm kept for an hour, being looked in on every twenty minutes. That's one way to get legroom on a flight these days.

Finally, in London, my girlfriend and I get to spend some time together before I have to head off again. Our goodbyes said (we'll be seeing each other again when this trip ends), I catch my flight to Yerevan, the capital of Armenia. Besides being cheated by a cab driver taking me from the airport to the hotel, my morning was relatively uneventful.

RUSSIANS AND CHRISTIANS

About a third of Armenia's population lives in its capital, Yerevan. Like many former Soviet cities, there is a stark efficiency to the area, though Yerevan certainly has its own style. One example of this is the Cascade, a five-story set of steps, fountains, and flower beds leading up to a monument commemorating the fiftieth anniversary of Soviet Armenia. Armenia gained its independence before the project could be completed, so it remains unfinished. The stairs present walkers with clear views of central Yerevan and Mount Ararat.

There's also Republic Square, which has a somewhat Roman feel in its design. The square consists of two sections: an oval roundabout with a stone pattern in the center, meant to resemble a traditional Armenian rug from above, and a trapezoid-shaped section containing a musical fountain in front of the History Museum and the National Gallery. During the Soviet period, it was called Lenin Square, and a statue of Vladimir Lenin stood there. After Armenia's independence, Lenin's statue was removed, and the square was renamed

After a nice lunch in a café near the opera house (where I had a fascinating take on a club sandwich), there's a drive west out to Echmiadzin. This is the holiest of sites for Armenian Christians, in part because it was the capital of Armenia when the country first adopted Christianity around 300 CE. Its main cathedral, Mayr Tachar, is surrounded by 19th-century buildings, though the entrance is quite modern.

The evening finds me skipping dinner in favor of an early night. I awaken fourteen hours later, finally caught up on some much-needed sleep.

BOOKS, GENOCIDE, AND DRIED FRUIT

Today begins with a visit to the Matenadaran Library, which houses over 17,000 Armenian manuscripts and 100,000 medieval and modern documents. Among the most significant manuscripts of the Matenadaran are the 9th-century Lazarian Gospel, the 10th-century Echmiadzin Gospel, and the 11th-century Mughni Gospel. The first, brought from the Lazarian Institute, is from 887 and is one of the library's oldest complete volumes. The Echmiadzin Gospel, dated from 989, has a 6th-century, possibly Byzantine, carved ivory cover. While the ancient manuscripts are remarkable, I became most interested in the exterior of the building and its remnants on display. I can never pass up photographing relics.

This is followed by a stop at a food market filled with many fresh and dried fruits varieties. While I try to make it through unscathed, I end up being stopped by an older man who keeps feeding me samples. Before I know what's hit me, I find myself the proud owner of a sample platter. Won't need to worry about snacks for a while. Across the street is the Blue Mosque, built-in 1765 by a Persian governor. It is one of the oldest surviving structures in central Yerevan and the most significant building from the city's Iranian period.

Next is Tsitsernakaberd, the Armenian Genocide Memorial and Museum. At the hands of the Ottoman Empire, an estimated 1.5 million Armenians were killed, as early as 1896 until as late as 1922. The museum is located underground and simply presents the facts, leaving viewers to make up their minds. At the end of the property is a towering monument and endless flame, where we each leave a white carnation.

TWO DAYS IN RUINS

A little more than an hour's drive east of Yerevan is Geghard Monastery, named after the holy lance that pierced Christ's side at the crucifixion (the actual lance is purportedly housed in Echmiadzin). Legend dates the monastery back to the 4th century. It is partially carved out of the adjacent mountain and surrounded by cliffs. Its interior is striking, though quite dark. As I do not travel with a tripod, I try my best to capture its essence handheld.

Nearby is Garni Temple, a Hellenistic temple initially constructed in the 1st century. It is the only standing Greco-Roman colonnaded building in Armenia (and the former Soviet Union) and is the best-known structure and symbol of pre-Christian Armenia. The temple has been restored and remains one of the few Pagan buildings still standing in Armenia. There are also remains of a Roman bathhouse a few feet away. Below the temple is a good hike revealing some fascinating rock formations.

Northwest of Yerevan can be found the fortress of Amberd, mostly dating from the 11th century. Its name translates to "fortress in the clouds." One can drive or hike there, which is my choice. The fortress remains are imposing, constructed on a ridge above the confluence of the Amberd and Arkashen streams. There is also a small church nearby, which is quite striking in its basalt construction. Along the way is the Park of Letters, displaying stone versions of the 39 letters of the Armenian alphabet. The alphabet was developed around 405 CE by Mesrop Mashtots, an Armenian linguist and ecclesiastical leader. The system originally had 36 letters; eventually, three more were adopted.

A DAY OF MONASTERIES

South of Yerevan, through the plains of Ararat, one finds Khor Virab Monastery. Mount Ararat rises behind the monastery, though today it is mostly concealed by clouds. It was here that St. Gregory was kept in a snake pit for 12 years before curing King Trdat III of insanity, resulting in the king's (and then the country's) conversion to Christianity. It is possible to visit the pit where Gregory was kept, though I decide to leave it to history. Northeast of the monastery is a lookout point offering some elevated views.

This is followed by Noravank Monastery, situated on the hill of a twisted gorge. The gorge is known for its tall, sheer, brick-red cliffs directly across from the monastery. The monastery is best known for its two-story Surb Astvatsatsin ("Holy Mother of God") church. Lunch is a picnic in a nearby cave, where I snap a few photos of the surrounding area. Heading north on the road over the Selim Pass, one comes across the Selim Caravanserai, a 14th-century travelers' inn along the Silk Road. Further on, one finds some lovely views of the pass and its Alpine meadows.

Rounding out the monasteries for the day is Sevan Monastery, high on a plateau overlooking Lake Sevan. Initially, the monastery was built at the southern shore of a small island. After the artificial draining of Lake Sevan, during the era of Joseph Stalin, the water level fell, and the island transformed into a peninsula. Originally constructed in the 9th century, by the 19th century the monastery was a place to reform wayward monks, enforcing a strict regime with no women allowed. Today it is one of the most visited tourist sights in Armenia.

INTO GEORGIA

My last day in Armenia begins in Dilijan. The town has preserved houses in it dating back to the 18th century along with another monument celebrating fifty years of Soviet Armenia, which has become the symbol of the town. On the way to Vanadzor, there is a Molokan village. Molokans are sectarian Christians who refused to obey the Russian Orthodox Church, beginning in the 1600s. In Vanadzor, a visit to its Black Church to witness a few moments of Sunday services.

Then on to Haghpat Monastery, a UNESCO World Heritage Site on account of its striking ecclesiastical architecture. The monastery is perched on the lip of the Debed Canyon and was founded around 976 by Queen Khosrvanuch. This is our last stop in Armenia, where I take my last Armenian photo.

For some reason, the group I'm traveling with decided that I should gather the tips for our Armenian guide and driver, who we will be leaving at the border. They also call on me to make a speech before presenting our guide and driver with their tips. Good thing years of teaching have taught me to improvise.

Border crossings are always tricky, but this one is not too bad. A stop at the end of Armenia to check my visa, stamp my passport, and say my goodbyes to our Armenia guide and driver. Then a short walk to the Georgian side to stamp my passport, x-ray my luggage, and check my passport again. Our Georgian guide is there to greet us and show us to our new transportation. It's about an hour's drive to Tbilisi and my first night in Georgia.

OLD THEN NEW

While Yerevan has not quite been able to shake all the remnants of its Soviet occupation, Tbilisi is a rather distinct European metropolis with little Soviet influence to be found. Around a third of Georgia's population of 4.4 million live in the capital, which is divided by the Mtkvari River. There is an Old Tbilisi and a New Tbilisi, which grew out from the old. Tbilisi means "warm spring," and the area is famous for its warm sulfur springs.

Overlooking the town is a large statue of Mother Georgia, holding a bowl of wine in one hand (for greeting friends) and a sword in the other (for greeting enemies). We begin our day by exploring Old Tbilisi, which has the impending Narikala Fortress perched above it. The fortress walls date from various periods, the earliest from the 4th century.

At one time, nearly 100,000 Jews lived in Tbilisi, a population that has now diminished to around 3000. There are two synagogues in town, the Great Synagogue, and the Little Synagogue. I explore the former, built from 1895 to 1903 in an eclectic style by Georgian Jews from Akhaltsikhe who migrated to Tbilisi in the late 19th century. From here, I head to a few more sites about town before wandering into New Tbilisi and back to the hotel for a much-needed shower and rest. Have I mentioned Georgia is experiencing a heatwave?

While my group had chosen me to collect tips and make a speech yesterday, in the evening our new guide selected me to gather everyone's passport at the hotel so she could make copies. I must have an honest face considering we'd only just met a few hours before, and the group that I've known for less than a week seemed eager to hand me their money and passports.

GOLDEN FLEECE (AND LEMONADE)

The town of Mtskheta is considered the spiritual heart of Georgia. One of the country's oldest cities and its former capital, it is located approximately 12 miles (20 km) north of Tbilisi. To get there, one takes a road that winds through narrow, forested valleys before dropping into the plains of the Rioni, Georgia's most important river. The city is overlooked by a 6th-century Jvari church. Below can be found what is considered the most sacred place in Georgia, the Svetitskhoveli Cathedral. The 9th-century basilica contains the grave of Sidonia, who was said to have been buried holding Christ's robe.

Arriving in Kutaisi, the ancient capital of the Kingdom of Colchis, we check into our guesthouse for a two-night stay. It was here that Jason stole the golden fleece from King Aeetes when he fell in love with the king's daughter, Medea. Kutaisi has always been an important town throughout the ages and for many years it was the capital of Georgia when the Arabs occupied Tbilisi.

My room is basic and hot, though I make-shift a way to keep the window open without the thin curtain being sucked out. I have earplugs in case this allows too much outside noise, though we are out of the main town, and I imagine it will be a quiet night. Dinner is quite a spread, and our hosts seem happy to have us.

While Jason was after the golden fleece (and the king's daughter), I have developed my own quest while in Georgia: lemonade. My first attempt brought me a fizzy pear-based drink. Yesterday's attempt resulted in a very green mint-based concoction. I will keep searching.

THE BAD SEA

As I have run out of imaginative ways to photograph churches, I've joined an excursion to Butami. Sitting on the southwest corner of Georgia, Butami is a port city on the Black Sea. While many seas (and islands, for that matter) seem to have gotten their name from pirates or long-ago adventurers, the Black Sea gets its name due to its notoriously rough waters and its propensity for sinking ships. Today, fortunately, its waters are calm.

Butami seems to have two major parts—the beach and the rest of town. I explore a little of both, with a stop for lunch in between. Here I again order lemonade and receive another fizzy pear drink. I might return from this trip with a craving for this previously unknown beverage. It's not lemonade, but it's not bad. In town, which has a somewhat colonial feel, there is a statue of Medea holding the golden fleece, which cost the country a controversial one million Georgian lari. That's a lot of lari. Her crown, necklace, and fleece all appear to be gold, which could account for some of the money.

About 6 miles (10 km) south of Batumi is the fortress of Gonio. Along with being a very large and well-preserved Roman fort, this is also believed to be the burial place of the apostle Matthias. According to the Acts of the Apostles, he was chosen by the apostles to replace Judas Iscariot following his betrayal of Jesus and subsequent death. His calling as an apostle is unique in that his appointment was not made personally by Jesus. There is a cross acknowledging his burial site, though the exact location remains unknown.

SACRIFICIAL LAMBS

Today, back to church. First up: Bagrati Cathedral, completed in 1003. It is presently undergoing renovation and is within walking distance from our guesthouse in Kutaisi. Bagrati was built by King Bagrat III, who united western and eastern Georgia. It is a masterwork of medieval Georgian architecture, though it has suffered heavy damage throughout the centuries and was reconstructed to its present state through a gradual process starting in the 1950s. Given the scaffolding, it appears the reconstruction continues.

This is followed by Motsameta Monastery, just 4 miles (6 km) out of Kutaisi. The monastery is situated on a cliff-top above a bend in the Tskhaltsitela River. Its name means "Place of the Martyrs," related to the brothers of a noble family who organized a rebellion against the occupying Arabs in the 8th century. When the rebellion failed, they were captured and promised forgiveness in exchange for converting to Islam. They declined, and their bodies were thrown into the river. It is here that I notice a lamb being taken from a car.

The monastery complex at Gelati was founded in 1106 by King David the Builder in gratitude to God for his victories over the Turks. The king wanted it to serve as a center of Christendom, and it was home to both scholars and religious artists. Here two more lambs are spotted, being walked around the main church. I ask my guide about this. She responds that when something special happens in some Georgian's lives, they bring a lamb to a nearby church to be blessed before sacrificing it.

CAVES, DESTRUCTION, AND SORE LEGS

Established by King Giorgi III in the 12th century as a stronghold against the Turkish Sultanate, Vardzia was developed by his daughter, Tamar. She created a cave monastery that became a center of Georgian culture. This network of caves above the Mtkvari river is rumored to have once numbered 3000, with up to 19 tiers in some places. Much of it was destroyed after a massive earthquake in 1456, and only 550 caves have been discovered spread over 13 levels. Numerous churches, meeting halls, refectories, and wine cellars are all interconnected by tunnels and stairways.

After hiking up to an excellent vantage point, our guide offers to take those interested into some of the caves. A handful of us agree, and I find myself contorting into some interesting shapes given the low roofs and covered stairways. Clearly, the inhabitants were not my height or weight. Coming down one of the stairways at an odd angle, I feel a pain where I've never felt one before in both of my legs, but it seems to pass after some time.

About a twenty-minute drive from Vardzia, one finds Khertvisi Fortress, situated on a cliff above the confluence of two major rivers. Built from the 10th to 14th centuries, its design features a square tower with rounded corners, unique in Georgia. It is a rough ascent after the hike to Vardzia, but I manage, ignoring my legs' adamant opposition. The church here was built in 985, and the existing walls were built in 1354. According to a local legend, Khertvisi was once destroyed by Alexander the Great, though it has been reconstructed and invaded on numerous occasions throughout the centuries.

NATIVE SON

In the morning, it's a ride on a "toy train," a two-car railroad on a narrow-gauge track going from Bakuriani to Borjomi, more or less. The construction of this line began in 1897 when Georgia was part of the Russian Empire. The arduous terrain caused construction to take four years, and the first train ran in January of 1902. After many days on a bus, it's a nice change of pace, though my aching legs don't like the narrow seating.

The town of Gori is famous for being the birthplace of Joseph Stalin, and they want everyone to know. In the square is a large, Soviet-era statue (one of the few Soviet-era statues remaining in Georgia) and around the corner a museum which includes another statue, Stalin's death mask, the home he was born in, and the train carriage he took to the Yalta Convention in 1945 (he didn't like flying).

Next up, more caves. Uplistsikhe features an entire town of streets, churches, palaces, and residential buildings carved into the mountainside. Dating from the first millennium BCE, it gradually grew to be an important city on the trade route linking Byzantium with India and China. It is notable for the unique mixture of various styles of rock-cut cultures from Anatolia and Iran, as well as the co-existence of pagan and Christian architecture.

A drive along the Georgia Military Highway takes us to Gudauri, settled into the Caucasus mountains in the north of the country. While heading to the Church of the Holy Trinity in Gergeti, there is a stop at a now ironic monument to 200 years of friendship between Georgia and Russia. There are also some beautiful views of the Kazbegi region along the way.

MY ACHING LEGS

To reach the Church of the Holy Trinity, one walks from Kazbegi town through Gergeti village. The trail is mainly along a dirt road, meaning that one gets covered in the dust generated by the jeeps going up and down (the option for those not wishing to walk). The hike up is quite beautiful, if unrelenting. I talk with our guide during the ascent and learn that she typically leads hiking tours, which explains why she has no problem with all of the trekking involved in the Georgian section of the trip. One of our group has somehow gotten it into his head that the guide and I are having an affair, and I'm sure our pairing up the mountain has only increased his suspicions.

The church itself is situated on a hilltop overlooking the snowy peaks of the Caucasus Mountains. Its isolated location on top of a steep mountain surrounded by the enormity of nature has made it a symbol for Georgia. In the distance is Mount Kazbegi, the highest peak in this region. It was here that, according to mythology, Prometheus was chained after giving mortals the gift of fire. There is also another lamb to be found, though this one seems quite content with its fate.

On the way back down, I snap a few final photos, but after three days of hiking, my legs have finally had it. On the way down from the church, I decide to take a shortcut, not realizing how steep and uneven the terrain is. Halfway down, my right calf cramps. I stop to massage it so that I can complete my descent, but I will be limping for the rest of the day. Tonight, I will buy a bottle of wine I've been eyeing at the hotel. While initially I wanted it more for the bottle than for the wine, now the wine seems an excellent idea.

GOODBYE, GEORGIA

About an hour's drive out of Gudauri, one finds Ananuri Fortress situated at the northwest end of the Zhinvali Reservoir. Within the fortress are two 17th century churches, the larger covered with stone carvings. Like many Georgian fortresses, it is striking and thankfully not high on a hill like so many other Georgian sites (my legs are still sore, I'm sorry to say).

Past Tbilisi on the way to Telavi is the town of Sighnahi. The town developed in the 18th century and has a distinctly Italian feel. The town is relatively small, and I spend my time shopping for a beverage and snack in a local market. Tonight, our last in Georgia, is a stay at another guesthouse, this time with a vast bedroom but a very poor shared bathroom. My group is spread over several homes, mine the furthest away. It's only myself and our guide in our house, providing more evidence of our imagined affair, I'm sure.

In the morning, there's the farmer's market in Telavi, where provisions for the day can be acquired. This is followed by a visit to Gremi Citadel, which stands on a small hill by the Telavi-Kvareli road. The complex is what has survived of the once flourishing town of Gremi. Its Church of the Archangels was constructed in 1565 and frescoed by 1577. Its design weds traditional Georgian masonry with a local interpretation of contemporary Iranian architectural taste. Here I take an assortment of color and black & white shots. These will prove to be my last Georgian photos as the border with Azerbaijan is less than an hour away.

NO COUNTRY FOR TALL MEN

There is a sign at the Azerbaijan border that in Georgian and English reads: Good Luck. The night before, our guide let us know that we might have difficulty crossing the border with anything Armenian, especially anything written in Armenian or containing information about the disputed Nagorno-Karabakh region. Luck was on my side as I was able to smuggle in a New Testament I'd picked up in Armenia, figuring it was a good souvenir as Armenia was the first Christian country. One of my group wasn't so lucky—his Lonely Planet guide was confiscated simply because it included Armenia. Most of us have the same book as it contains the three countries together, though his was the only one filled with notes.

While a new guide is awaiting us across the border, our Georgian guide stays on as a coordinator. Let the imagined affair continue. Our first day in Azerbaijan is spent in the town of Shaki. We're staying at a converted caravanserai, which requires ducking to get to my room. I explore a bit of the old town, passing an old man with a stuffed wolf (it's rumored he'll light up the wolf's plastic eyes for one manat). One of Shaki's attractions is Khan's Palace, built-in 1797 by Muhammed Hasan Khan, which requires ducking to get into its many rooms.

Nearby is the village of Kis, where one can find a renovated Albanian church. Caucasian Albania was the Christian nation that once covered most of northern Azerbaijan. The courtyard to the church has a very low door—I'm noticing a pattern here. After exploring the village, there is time for an excellent coffee in a café, where I am photographically inspired by the yellow and pink sugar cubes.

BAKU BOUND

It is a long drive from Shaki to Baku. Along the way, one passes through Samaxi, once one of northern Azerbaijan's most prominent cities. We're here to visit the Yedid Gumbaz Mausoleum, also known as Seven Domes due to the seven domed mausoleums built within the cemetery. Here the family of the Mustafa Khan, the last ruler of Shamakhi khanate, have been buried. Only three of the seven original mausoleums have survived without being damaged over the years. The other mausoleums have been partially damaged, some losing their domes and walls.

The history of Baku is long, with one of its most recent entries being its oil boom of the early 20th century, when Azerbaijan produced more than half the world's supply of oil and its capital, Baku, grew uncontrollably. Now there are high-end shops, five-star hotels, and the police drive 3-series BMWs. Contrasted with this, the old city is filled with historic mosques, caravanserais, and traditional wooden balconies, all preceding the boom.

Wandering about town, we come across the Shirvanshah Palace complex, parts of which date back to the 15th century. The palace was partly destroyed in the 18th century by the Russians, but reconstruction work was carried out to restore the complex to its original state. In the afternoon, we make a to visit the Atesgah ("Fire Temple") of Baku. Based on Persian and Indian inscriptions, the temple was used as a Hindu, Sikh, and Zoroastrian place of worship. Fire rituals at the area's numerous natural gas vents date back to at least the 10th century, though this complex was built during the 17th and 18th centuries. It was abandoned in the late 19th century. Its natural eternal flame went out in 1969 and is now lit by gas piped from the nearby city.

CAESAR GERMANICUS WAS HERE

About an hour's drive south of Baku, one comes across the petroglyphs of Qobustan, which date back to the Iron and Stone Ages. The site was discovered by accident when a group of men went there to quarry for stone in 1930. It has more than 6000 rock carvings depicting people, animals, ritual dances, warriors with spears in their hands, camel caravans, along with pictures of the sun and stars. Nearby is some graffiti etched by a Roman soldier—said to be the easternmost Latin inscription yet found. The inscription translates as: "Emperor Domitianus, the Blessed Caesar Germanicus. Livius Maximus, Legio XII Fulminata." There is only one stone with an inscription, but I do my best to make the photos interesting.

Also in this region are dozens of so-called "mud volcanoes" no more than a few feet high. Azerbaijan has the most mud volcanoes of any country, spread across the country. In fact, half of the mud volcanoes of the world are found in the Azerbaijani Republic. They emit cold mud, water, and gas almost continually, creating a strangely beautiful sight. While most of us are careful in wondering about the area, one of our group ends up thigh deep in one of the volcanoes. Fortunately for them, they emit cold mud.

In the evening, our group has its final meal together. The one in our group who has imagined my affair with our Georgian guide asks if he can bring his tip for her to me before we depart the hotel for dinner as he won't be joining us. I give him my room number and note that it's the room next to hers. "Of course, it is," he replies with a wry smile. Guess I won't be setting the record straight with him this trip.

Jun. 2010 – *Western Balkans*

After just two days in London following my Southern Caucasus trip, I'm on the road again. This time it's the Western Balkans: Croatia, Montenegro, and Bosnia and Herzegovina. This trip is a little different. First, rather than traveling on my own, I'm with my future wife. Second, there's no tour this time; it's all on our own. We had found a tour we liked but realized we could easily do it on our own. This will become a template in the future, where we keep an eye out for tours to borrow their routes and itineraries. We've booked a flight from London to Dubrovnik, where we have rented an apartment for the week. Then it's a local bus to Sarajevo for two nights in a hotel followed by another bus to Split for our final two nights.

DOMESTIC IN DUBROVNIK

As our flight to Dubrovnik leaves early and a taxi would cost too much, we decide to spend the night in the airport. Usually, I would avoid this situation at all costs, but I figure it's another change to my usual way of travel. That, of course, doesn't mean that I won't still complain about it. I can also now report that along with airplanes, I also can't sleep in airports.

Our flight is uneventful, and we arrive in Dubrovnik in the early afternoon. Once at baggage claim, I give Boris, our apartment owner, a call and he explains to a cab driver how to find his place. The road from the airport to Dubrovnik is along the coast, and I can say that the Croatian coast, at least in the south, is simply stunning. The landscape is lush with isolated coves enhanced with azure waters and sandy beaches.

Our apartment is quite lovely, with a separate kitchen and bathroom. The idea of renting an apartment for the week is that we can make our own breakfast in the mornings and cook the occasional dinner. And we have a garden terrace overlooking the Adriatic Sea where we can eat our meals, should we choose. Now I just need to figure out how to use this odd remote for the air conditioning.

Once settled, we head into the old town for dinner. Everywhere seems to be pizza, pasta, or seafood, which is not surprising as this area was under Venetian rule for centuries. We also look for a market to buy provisions for the week. Thankfully there is one just down from our apartment, though it is quite the climb from the road up. We'll have plenty of time to explore the area more fully in the coming days.

THE BLACK MOUNTAINS

Before departing on this Balkans trip, we found some day trips from Dubrovnik, which we booked in advance. Our first is a day trip into Montenegro, which my guidebook describes as being known for its incredible beauty. Once all the assorted passengers are picked up (we were picked up at a nearby hotel), our first stop is along the Bay of Kotor before heading into Kotor proper and its old town. Here we stop in a nearby café for refreshments before exploring the town.

The old Mediterranean port of Kotor is surrounded by fortifications erected during the Venetian period. Some have called the Bay of Kotor the southernmost fjord in Europe, though it is, in reality, a submerged river canyon. Together with the overhanging limestone cliffs, Kotor and its surrounding area form an impressive landscape.

Before a dip inland into Cetinje, the secondary capital of Montenegro, and the official residence of the president, we have a lunch of local ham and cheese sandwiches, and I attempt the honey wine, which is quite refreshing. We both end up taking several photos of a nearby cow while also trying to capture the tiny residential cabins in the background. I swear the cow started posing at one point.

Our last stop of the day is a return to the coast and a stop in Budva, which is 2500 years old, making it one of the oldest settlements on the Adriatic Sea coast. The coastal area around Budva, referred to as the Budva riviera, is the center of Montenegrin tourism, known for its well-preserved medieval walled city, sandy beaches, and diverse nightlife. After some exploration, we take a ferry ride back to the Bay of Kotor and return to Dubrovnik.

AN INADVERTENT WINK

Today is supposed to be a day trip into Mostar, Bosnia and Herzegovina, famous for its Old Bridge. But by 7:45 a.m. our 7:30 a.m. bus has not arrived to pick us up. So, I call the number on my pre-paid voucher only to be told that this tour only runs on Saturdays, not Thursdays. "But my voucher clearly states Thursday on it," I explain. "That does not matter," I am told, "this tour only runs on Saturdays." This back and forth continues for a while before I give up the fight and switch the pickup to Saturday. "Will they accept my Thursday voucher as I cannot print another?" I ask. "The tour only runs on Saturdays," comes the response. I guess we'll have to wait and see. I had planned a free day in Dubrovnik on Saturday, so we'll move that to today.

We head from our failed pickup location into the old town, figuring it's early enough for the lighting to be good and for there to be fewer people, at least fewer tourists, in the streets. The old town is surrounded by ancient walls that tourists seem to like to climb only during the heat of the day. There are also several churches, a clock tower, and a few fountains to be found. While heading to a fruit market, I inadvertently wink at a passing nun, who smiles, so I'm guessing it's not too bad of a sin.

Dubrovnik's Old Town is known as one of the world's most perfectly preserved medieval cities in the world. For centuries, Dubrovnik itself rivaled Venice as a trading port, with its vast stone walls, built between the 11th and 17th centuries, affording protection. After exploring, we have a leisurely afternoon back at our apartment where H (name withheld to protect the innocent) makes a light lunch, and we escape the heat of the day with a nap. I can get into this local apartment living.

LONG DRIVE TO A SMALL ISLAND

Today is another day trip that we nearly miss. My voucher says the pickup is at 7:30 a.m., but at 7:20 a.m. the bus is getting ready to leave. The driver tells us the pickup was at 7:15 a.m. and I don't see the point of arguing, as clearly any information on my vouchers are not reliable. We are heading to Korcula Island, the alleged hometown of Marco Polo, which is a lengthy drive (followed by a ferry ride) from Dubrovnik. This island is the most populous Croatian island not connected to the mainland by a bridge, hence the need for a ferry.

The old town of Korcula is small and, like all the old towns we've been to so far, situated along the coast. Unlike the other old towns we've been to this trip, this one is laid out in the shape of a fish's skeleton with only one north-south road intersected by curving east-west roads that allow for natural air-conditioning. Located on a small peninsula, the town is still surrounded by thick 14th century stone walls and towers built in medieval times for defense.

On the drive back, we make a stop in Ston, which contains the second-longest continuous ancient wall in the world (Hadrian's Wall in northern England would be the second-longest after China's Great Wall if it were still continuous). Originally more than 4.3 miles (7 km) in length, Ston's walls are the longest defensive structure in Europe, sometimes referred to as the "European Walls of China."

Upon our return to Dubrovnik, I take a photo I've been eyeing since we arrived. I keep waiting for the right light but only seem to pass the spot either early in the morning, when the lighting is not great, or well into the evening when there is no light.

BOSNIA TIMES THREE

There is an enclave along the Croatian coast, which belongs to Bosnia and Herzegovina. Since 1991 and the breakup of Yugoslavia, the borders between Croatia and Bosnia and Herzegovina in this region have been international borders. This means that to get to Mostar and back, we cross the border between these two countries three times. The first crossing takes us into this enclave and the small town of Neum, our first official stop in Bosnia. During our morning stop here, there is one battleship in the bay; upon our return in the early evening, there are two.

Then we're back in Croatia only to return to Bosnia a few miles later. Fortunately, while the officials do look at everyone's passports, they are not stamping our passports, or they'd quickly be filled with Croatian and Bosnian entry and exit stamps. Our second stop in Bosnia is Pocitelj, where we buy some cherries for the remaining drive to Mostar.

Mostar is the biggest and the most important city in the Herzegovina region. Between 1992 and 1993, after Bosnia and Herzegovina declared independence from Yugoslavia, the town was subject to an 18-month siege. There are still signs of this attack, including wreckage on display with "Remember" painted beneath it. There are also several bullet-riddled walls on display. Its famous arched Old Bridge was destroyed, though it has been reconstructed.

After exploring the town, we find a picturesque café where we order a meat platter to share. Given Dubrovnik's limited menu options, at least in the Old Town, it's a nice change of pace, and the outdoor setting allows for some beautiful views of the town along with some opportunities to people watch.

SLIGHT CHANGE OF PLANS

There was a knock at our door last night. Boris, our apartment's owner, is there to inform us that a regular guest of his is arriving the following day and she always stays in our apartment. Not to worry, he assures us, he has lined up a room for us for our last night with neighbors who have just started renting rooms to tourists and, if we can leave our packed bags at our front door in the morning, he will collect them before cleaning the room, and we can collect them from him when we return for the day. He will then introduce us to our new family for the night.

All this seems odd, considering he shouldn't have let us book knowing someone else was arriving before our visit came to an end. Still, I'm learning not to question things in this region as everyone seems to accept that things are as they are regardless of logic or what's printed on a voucher. So, we pack our bags and leave them out for Boris to collect before heading out to be picked up for our day trip to Mostar.

Upon our return, we head back to our old apartment, say hello to the new tenant enjoying the outdoor seating, and gather our bags from Boris. He then escorts us to our new home for the night. The wife greets us. We need to make our way through the main entrance and up a flight of stairs to our room. The house is dark, and our room is small, but it will do as we have an early morning to catch our bus to Sarajevo.

Speaking of which, after dropping off our bags, we make our way to the bus station, where through mimicry and hand gestures, H is able to procure our tickets for the following morning.

SMALL TOWN SARAJEVO

It's a nearly seven-hour bus ride from Dubrovnik to Sarajevo, with two more border crossings. We find an informative cab driver who takes us from the bus station to our hotel while giving us a very detailed tour along the way. He was in Sarajevo when the Serbs were firing into town on a daily basis. "They were shooting into town from those hills," he'd tell us. "See that market," he said, pointing while driving, "it was bombed. Thirty people killed."

As we'd taken a local bus, English was not spoken, and we were not sure when a break was to stretch our legs or to have lunch. As such, we arrive in Sarajevo very hungry. When telling her of our plight, the receptionist at our hotel suggests a restaurant around the corner that she says is popular with tourists. The waiter there seems a little surprised when we order three meals to share.

Sarajevo is not an attractive city, I'm sorry to say, at least not the way we entered it. I was secretly hoping that we'd arrived in the wrong town at first, that this mistake would be revealed, and the right town would be found only a few miles away. Its old town is charming, though relatively small. It is raining during our morning of exploration, so we seek refuge in a café for about an hour before the rain finally passes.

We explore for a bit more, then realize that we've pretty much seen all that we can as we walk down the same streets for the fourth time. In Mostar, I saw old pocket watches for sale and found one here that I like, but it is far too expensive for a souvenir. I never come to a country seeking a particular souvenir. I just wonder about and see if something catches my eye.

TWO NIGHTS IN SPLIT

A few years ago, at the Palm Springs Film Festival, I saw a Croatian movie that was shot in the town of Split. Ever since I have wanted to head there with my camera. Well, today we're heading to Split. Initially, it took some persuading to talk H into it, but, as it turns out, Split is possibly the highlight of the trip. Guess I should have shown her the film.

The bus from Sarajevo to Split is eight hours, though we planned better this time and had a bounty of provisions with us. We pass through some stunning scenery that I would like to return to someday on foot to explore fully as I can only admire it from the bus. When we arrive at the bus terminal in Split, we get another taxi to what we think is our hotel, only to discover that I've rented an apartment a bit of a climb from the main square. The neighborhood is nice, with children playing and friendly dogs roaming, though I'm beginning to think I should have left a trail of something back into town as we head higher and higher.

In the morning, we explore the town. Of all the old towns we've seen this trip, Split is undoubtedly the most beautiful. Most famous in the city is Diocletian's Palace, built for the Roman emperor Diocletian at the turn of the 4th century, which today forms about half the old town of Split. The term "palace" is misleading as the structure is enormous and resembles a large fortress. About half of it was for Diocletian's personal use, while the other half housed a military garrison. Located at the southern end of the palace are the "basement halls" that held the private apartments of Diocletian and represent one of the best-preserved ancient complexes of their kind. There is also a promenade along the port filled with day-trippers and over-priced food.

RUINS FOR A CHANGE

As if persuading H to come to Split was not hard enough, I discover some nearby ruins in the town of Solin that she's really uncertain about. As I only have my guidebook's sparse description to go by (not even one photo to help strengthen my case), I use the selling point that "at least it's not another old town." That works, and we hop a taxi.

Solin developed on the site of the ancient city of Salona, which was the capital of the Roman province of Dalmatia and the birthplace of Emperor Diocletian (of the famous palace). When the cab driver drops us off, I'm immediately drawn to the Manastirine, which served as a burial place for early Christians. To be honest, I think this is the whole site and take my time exploring until H discovers that there's far more to be seen, so we'll need to be quick as our cab is returning in an hour to retrieve us.

After purchasing our tickets to enter the proper site, a path bordered by cypress trees takes us to ruins that include a cathedral, baptistery, and public baths. H gets distracted by a friendly dog, so I leave her to look for more ruins. On the way back, I reunite with H. Soon, a group of local women call after me as they've retrieved my wayward hat that flew off my head in the rush to get back to the entrance and our hopefully awaiting taxi. I hadn't even noticed.

Upon our return to Split, we explore the city a little more as it is terribly photogenic. In the morning, it's another airport and a short flight back to London. I've been on the go for five weeks so far and am looking forward to settling down for a bit and finally getting to explore London properly.

Jul. 2010 – *London, Venice, and Brussels*

Now that my two major trips this summer were over, I spent the rest of my break in London. My girlfriend H and I borrowed a studio apartment from a friend of hers near Regent's Park, which will be our base till my return to the U.S. in August. Along with London, we've also planned a weekend in Venice and a weekend in Belgium. H has been to both, but I have not, and she has agreed to return to both with me. And there are some day trips from London. Together we're heading to Brighton, Cambridge, and Hampton Court. While H is at work, I'll be heading out to St. Albans, Bath, Salisbury, and Stonehenge. It was during this trip, while in London, that I proposed to H and she accepted.

AN AMERICAN TOURIST IN LONDON

On our first night back from the Balkans, we have dinner with H's mother and decide to have some cocktails after. When H and her mom travel, they tend to buy alcohol that they don't really drink after. We start with a gin and tonic (using proper British gin) followed by rum and coke (using a Cuban rum I've been eyeing since I first was in her mom's place). Then it's a sampling of a chocolate-flavored brandy from Israel and a cherry liqueur we brought back from Croatia. We then finish the night with coffee and a cream liqueur. We will all be sleeping well tonight.

It's been thirty-three days since I left my California home and headed for London (and six other countries). Today is my first day as a tourist, seeing the main sights all tourists come to see. As this is H's town, I let her take the lead. First up: A train to Waterloo Station followed by the London Eye, which I become a little photographically obsessed with. This is followed by a stroll down to Westminster Bridge and my first glimpses of Big Ben and the Houses of Parliament. It's high season for tourists, and they are out in abundance. Why is it they always stop in the middle of the road to check their maps?

We explore a bit more of Westminster before heading to St. James' Park, where we spend an hour having a lunch packed by H on deck chairs surrounded by office workers sunning themselves on the grass (some in bikinis). We then resume our exploration, heading to Buckingham Palace, home to the British monarchy since Queen Victoria took up residence in 1837. Here I do my best to capture a decent photo of a Royal Guard. We end our day at Piccadilly Circus, where we eventually make our way to the tube and back to our apartment.

CAMERA CONFUSION

This morning I'm off to explore on my own before meeting H for lunch. I get off at the Holborn Tube Station and head down along Great Queen Street to Long Acre. In the area is a wonderful bookstore specializing in travel books I spend some time in (wondering how many books I should be considering purchasing as I will need to pack them when I leave). I have noticed that London bookshops often have specials—buy three, get the fourth free, for instance—and I enjoy that the price on the sticker is the price one pays. The price in the U.S. is always before sales tax, and the sales tax varies depending upon which state and county you are in. I also wander past the busy Covent Garden tube station before entering Covent Garden.

Here I meet H, and we head off for a lunch of Cornish pasties at a location recommended by friends. It's not bad, though I find the fold a bit thick. It may be traditional, but we're no longer coal miners needing a place to grip and not eat. Afterward, we explore the area for a bit. Both of us take photos with my camera, so I try to keep a mental note of who took what photo. We head to Neal's Yard, a rather bohemian area filled with brightly colored buildings and vegetarian restaurants.

Then I'm back on my own and head to Temple district, owned by the Knights Templar from 1185-1312. It was also at the Middle Temple Hall where Shakespeare's *Twelfth Night* debuted in 1600. As I leave, I get excited to see a large bookshop on a corner before realizing that it's a law bookstore. So instead of buying books, I snap a few last photos in the area before calling it a day.

BRIGHTON IN PRINT AND ON FILM

One of my mom's favorite authors is Agatha Christie. One of my first introductions to Brighton was as a setting for a Hercule Poirot mystery. Was there ever a better Poirot than David Suchet? Later it served as a backdrop to Graham Greene's early novel, *Brighton Rock*. The area emerged as a health resort featuring sea bathing during the 18th century. It became a destination for day-trippers after the arrival of the railway in 1841. Today over eight million tourists a year visit Brighton.

It's a pleasant train ride from London to Brighton, and we begin our exploration with the main town, filled with quaint shops and eateries. We then head to the Royal Pavilion, built in the Indo-Saracenic style prevalent in India for most of the 19th century. It was built in three campaigns, beginning in 1787, as a seaside retreat for George, Prince of Wales, later to become George IV. Successors William IV and Victoria also used the Pavilion, but Queen Victoria decided that Osborne House on the Isle of Wight should be the royal seaside retreat, and the Pavilion was sold to the city of Brighton in 1850.

Then it's on to the beach, where everyone comes here for. Unlike my familiar scantily clad southern California beaches, Brighton has a proper British feel, with modestly dressed bathers along with very butch seagulls. On the pier, H and I take a rest before heading for tea and scones. I'm not sure if these scones are typical of England, but they are huge. I wonder if they are this big in Brighton in order to defend oneself from the butch seagulls that seem to be on the lookout for any unguarded food. Might explain their physique.

USE YOUR IMAGINATION

It's my birthday, and I've decided to start the day with an archeological walking tour of Roman London. I enjoy walking and archeology—what could possibly go wrong?

Well, first off, there is very little left to see of Roman London—it's all been built over. So, we spend the first thirty minutes of our walking tour standing in front of St. Paul's tube station talking about what was found underneath buildings in the area during their constructions or renovations. I get restless and take a few photos of the area while our guide rambles on.

Have I mentioned it's been a half-hour and we haven't walked yet? We finally set off and, wait for it—there are actually some ruins that were revealed after bombings during the Second World War. This is followed by Guildhall Yard, once home to a Roman amphitheater. Then it's on to Moorgate and the remains of a Roman city wall. The Romans first built the defensive London Wall around the port town of Londinium about 200 CE. From the 18th century onward, the expansion of the City of London saw large parts of the wall demolished, including its city gates, to improve traffic flow. Other parts of the wall were incorporated into new or existing buildings.

This ends our tour, so H and I head out on our own. First, some photos of the City of London, which is London's primary central business district. Then on to St. Paul's Cathedral. A Roman temple to Diana may once have stood on the site, though the first Christian cathedral there was dedicated to St. Paul in 604 CE. We cross the Millennium Bridge and walk a bit along Bankside.

So, when do I get my presents?

VENETIAN WEEKEND: FRIDAY

Initially, we were going to be spending my birthday weekend in Venice but, as we'd recently returned from the Balkans, we decided to postpone till the following weekend to give us a little more time to recharge. That weekend has arrived, and it's an early wake-up and taxi ride to the airport followed by a short flight and a water bus to the San Marco pier. Our hotel is only a short walk away.

From the 5th to 8th centuries, Huns, Goths, and assorted barbarians repeatedly sacked Roman towns along Veneto's Adriatic coast. Venetian settlers rose above their swampy circumstances and established terra firma with wood pylons driven into some 100 feet (30 meters) of silt. Add a thousand or so additional years, and Venice has become one of the must-see cities of Europe, filled with the world's most artistic masterpieces per square mile.

After settling into our room, we set off to explore San Marco. Our hotel is right outside of the Piazza San Marco, so we start there. Piazza San Marco, also referred to as St Mark's Square, is the principal public square of Venice. It contains the city's most famous buildings, including St Mark's Basilica and the Doge's Palace. Napoleon is reputed to have called the plaza "the world's most beautiful drawing-room." This is where all the tourists and cruise ship day-trippers head, and it can be quite congested.

After a bit of time along the coast, we head inland. H has the map, so I leave it to her to maneuver the many twists and turns to be found here. One can quickly tell that this was an area added on to rather than formally designed as many roads lead to dead-ends.

VENETIAN WEEKEND: SATURDAY

This morning we explore a bit more of San Marco before heading to the Rialto Bridge, which is a challenge to photograph with all the tourists on it being photographed. This seems to be true of almost every bridge in Venice—either people stop on them to get their photo taken or to check their maps. There also seems always to be a gondolier or two sitting on the railing proclaiming, "Gondola, gondola!" The Rialto, of course, is not just any bridge—it connects San Marco with San Polo, our next destination.

San Polo is the smallest and most central of the six sestieri of Venice. It is one of the city's oldest parts, having been settled before the 9th century, and is named for the Church of San Polo. While exploring, we discover a Chinese restaurant that will serve as our choice for dinner. It is a hot day, and there are many narrow roads with tall buildings and no ventilation. We come across a small square with a breeze, so we stop for drinks along a canal and watch the world go by for a while.

Then it's the Accademia Bridge for a dip into Dorsoduro, which we will explore more fully in the morning. In a city of magnificent stone architecture, it is unusual to come across a large, plain wooden bridge. Along with a break from all the stone, it also happens to offer two of the best views in Venice, looking along the Grand Canal in each direction. We explore a bit before heading back to our hotel to refresh. Our room may be small, but it offers excellent and much-needed air conditioning. In the evening, it's on to the Chinese restaurant, which seems to employ the entire Chinese population of Venice if our five servers are any indication.

VENETIAN WEEKEND: SUNDAY

This morning we hail a water bus over to Lido, the island setting of Thomas Mann's *Death in Venice*. Besides the beach, there is not much to see in Lido, though it is refreshing to find cars on the road. Here we stop for an early lunch before wandering down the main avenue. I had hoped to walk over to Antico Cimitero Israelitico, the Jewish Cemetery, but it is too hot and stagnant to even contemplate. So, we head to the beach for a quick look around then walk immediately back to the water bus station.

We're dropped off in Dorsoduro, which we only saw a bit of yesterday. There is a calmness here that one does not find in San Marco, with far fewer tourists and much quieter streets. Walking here takes one through humble workers' areas to boisterous student quarters to peaceful luxury dwellings. Dorsoduro is also home to some of the most impressive art collections, including the Peggy Guggenheim Collection located within the palazzo Venier dei Leoni. I'm not sure if I am more impressed with the art or the palazzo. Guggenheim purchased the palazzo and the garden behind it in 1949 and made it her home for the following thirty years. In 1951, Guggenheim began to open her home and collection to the public, free of charge, three afternoons a week from Easter to November, and continued to do so until her death in 1979. After our visit, we return for a last few moments in San Marco before heading to catch our water bus back to the airport.

At the airport, we discover we've been upgraded and are now allowed into the Marco Polo Lounge. Had we known, we would have arrived with more than half an hour to spare. I find myself appreciative of the added legroom on the return flight and being trusted with metal cutlery.

ST. ALBANS AND VERULAMIUM

St. Albans was a settlement of pre-Roman origin named Verlamion, now located in southern Hertfordshire. It became the first major town on the old Roman road of Watling Street for travelers heading north and developed into the Roman city of Verulamium. Saint Alban, the first British Christian martyr, was beheaded here sometime before 324 CE and gave the town its current name.

Today I am on a day trip to see what little remains of the Roman Verulamium. I've joined my group at the train station, where we buy return tickets. After arriving, we explore the modern town a bit. St. Albans has the distinction of having memorials listing those killed during WWI on the streets on which the soldiers lived. In all, there are thirteen. St. Albans is also noted for having the most pubs per square mile in Britain.

The best-preserved Roman ruins are a theater and outlines of some businesses. Although there are other Roman theaters in Britain, the one at St. Albans is claimed to be the only example of its kind, being a theater with a stage rather than an amphitheater. The theater was built around 140 CE. While urban life continued in Verulamium into the 5th century, the theater had fallen into neglect by that time. It was used as a rubbish dump in the 4th century and was excavated in the 19th century and again in the 1930s.

Next up is St. Michael's church, a possible location of Saint Alban's trial. This is followed by a park where one can find a Roman mosaic and remnants of a wall and gate. Our last stop is St. Albans Abbey, originally constructed of Roman bricks. This was the location of Saint Alban's execution.

THE BRIDGES OF CAM

The University of Cambridge is the second oldest university in England and the fourth oldest in the world. The university was founded in 1209 when academics escaping hostility in Oxford fled to the area. It is composed of 31 colleges, and its oldest existing college, Peterhouse, was founded in 1284. Settlements in the area of Cambridge itself, along the river Cam, have existed before the Roman Empire. As an academic, I am always interested in college towns, and H has been kind enough to offer to take me here. As a fan of Inspector Morse, I'm also hoping to visit Oxford someday.

We begin our exploration by walking down from the train station, passing an assemblage of schools and businesses. This leads us to St. John's College, whose alumni include nine Nobel Prize winners, six Prime Ministers, and three Saints. Founded as a men's college in 1555, it has been coeducational since 1979. It was established to provide a source of educated Roman Catholic clerics to support the Counter-Reformation under Queen Mary. We plan on following this with Trinity College, but it is closed to visitors today. So instead, we go on a punting tour, passing seven of the colleges from the river.

We follow our boating adventure with a visit to Clare College, recommended by our punter. The college was founded in 1326 as University Hall, making it the second-oldest surviving college after Peterhouse. We also attempt King's College, but it is closed for a wedding. In fact, many of the colleges are closed today for various graduations and other ceremonies. This doesn't stop us from exploring a bit more of the town before hopping the train back.

HAMPTON COURT GARDENS

Hampton Court Palace is a royal residence in southwest London, though it has not been lived in by the British Royal family since the 18th century. Originally built for Cardinal Wolsey by King Henry VIII around 1514, the palace passed on to the king when Wolsey fell from favor. King William III began massive rebuilding and expansion work in the following century, intending to rival the Palace of Versailles. His work concluded in 1694, leaving the palace in two contrasting architectural styles: domestic Tudor and Baroque. But today is not about palaces, it's about gardens, and Hampton Court has some remarkable ones.

While there are many gardens to explore here, H and I set off for the vast Great Fountain Garden. William III and Mary II created the Great Fountain Garden on the East Front to complement their elegant new Baroque palace. After being opened to the public by Queen Victoria in 1838, the Great Fountain Garden became the highlight of a visit to Hampton Court Palace. I busy myself with some photos around the perimeter, along with some creative shots within the fountain itself. Who needs Jackson Pollock when there's pond scum to zoom in on?

Then we move into the Privy Garden, a re-creation based on a 1701 design made for William III, who didn't live to enjoy his new garden. In 1702, he fell from his horse and died two weeks later. During Henry VIII's day, this served as the king's private garden, and it remained a private garden for residents of the palace until the early 20th century. From here, we wander about a bit more, taking various photos, where I am blissfully ignorant of exactly which garden I'm looking at.

BELGIUM GETAWAY: FRIDAY

It seems that Hercule Poirot is in the air, first with our visit to Brighton and now with a weekend stop in Belgium. The country was a founding member of the European Union and houses its headquarters, along with many other international organizations, such as NATO. While H has been here before, I never have and would particularly like to see Bruges. We decide to stay in Brussels and plan a day trip out to Ghent and Bruges.

We catch the Eurostar from London to Brussels, stopping in Lille after going under the Channel. I have always found trains more comfortable than planes or buses for the mere fact that one has the option to walk about, even if one does not need to. You can technically walk on a plane, but I'm often on red-eye flights and don't want to disturb those trying to sleep. And you get to enjoy the view on a train. The Lille to Brussels portion of the ride also serves the most decadently amazing hot chocolate, giving it another plus.

After navigating our way through the Brussels underground system, we settle into our hotel before heading to the central square, Grand Place. It is surrounded by opulent Baroque guildhalls of the former Guilds of Brussels and two larger edifices—the city's extravagant Town Hall and the neo-Gothic King's House. This is one of those locations that is frustratingly beautiful as it is nearly impossible to capture on camera. This doesn't mean that I won't try over the next three days. I do find myself stepping further and further back into corners to try to capture more and begin to realize it may be time to start looking into purchasing a wide-angle lens.

BELGIUM GETAWAY: SATURDAY

Today is our day trip to Ghent and Bruges. We get up early and head for some breakfast. While our hotel is very nice and centrally located, it does lack breakfast. With not much open, we stop for coffee and pastries before getting in a morning view of Grand Place. I am determined to capture the grandness this location on camera somehow.

Ghent is located in the Flemish region of Belgium. In the Middle Ages it was one of the largest and wealthiest cities in northern Europe. The city originally started as a settlement at the convergence of the Rivers Scheldt and Leie and, in the Late Middle Ages, became one of the largest and wealthiest cities of northern Europe, with over 50,000 people in 1300. We are here during Gentse Feesten, a ten-day music and theater festival, so tents and banners obstruct some views. We begin our walking tour at the Saint Nicholas Church, besides the Belfry and Saint Bavo Cathedral. Then into more of the town. While Ghent is Belgium's second-largest municipality, it remains quaint and unrushed.

Bruges is a canal-based city in the shape of an egg and maintains most of its medieval architecture. Along with a few other canal-based northern cities, such as Amsterdam and St. Petersburg, it is sometimes referred to as the "Venice of the North." The Church of Our Lady is one of the world's largest bricks towers/buildings and houses the only statue by Michelangelo that left Italy during his lifetime. Bruges' most famous landmark is the Belfry, a 13th-century belltower housing a carillon comprising 47 bells. The city still employs a full-time carillonneur, who gives free concerts regularly. We then explore the old city center, making way for the frequent horse-drawn carriages.

BELGIUM GETAWAY: SUNDAY

Today, H and I set out to explore more of Brussels before our train ride back to London. We have a map and H's memory of her time here before to guide us. As we wander about, I take various photos and seem to have a particular interest in architectural details today, which Brussels has in abundance. If I can't capture it in wide-angle, then I can at least zoom in to capture some of the intricate details that abound.

Brussels has an odd landmark: A bronze fountain statue of a young boy peeing known as "Manneken Pis," installed around 1618. H has been on and on about this statue since our arrival, so much so that I begin to contemplate an intervention upon our return. But it seems that the whole city is obsessed. Likenesses of the statue are everywhere: on postcards, as magnets, even in assorted chocolates. When we finally come across it, I'm all for skipping the photography, but H won't let that happen, so I snap a photo, and we're on our way.

As all is fair in love and urination, I decide we should look up "Jeanneke Pis," Manneken's female counterpart. Jeanneke is a modern fountain sculpture commissioned in 1985 and completed in 1987. The 20-inch (50 cm) bronze statue depicts a little girl with her hair in short pigtails, squatting and urinating on a blue-grey limestone base. If I wanted to complete the trifecta, there is also "Zenneke Piss," a sculpture of a urinating dog, but I've reached my limit on weeing statues for the day.

Finally, checked out of our hotel, it's the underground to Gare du Midi to catch our train back to London. To my knowledge, none of its landmarks urinate.

SALISBURY AND STONEHENGE

In Greek, the name for a bishop's chair is a "cathedra," and any church containing a cathedra is designated a cathedral. Historically, in Europe, a city was understood to be an urban settlement if it had a cathedral. With this in mind, today I'm off on my own to Salisbury, a city known for its stunning cathedral.

I explore some of the town before heading into the cathedral itself, completed in 1258. Its 404 feet (123 meter) tall spire, built-in 1320, has been the tallest church spire in the United Kingdom since 1561. While I usually don't photograph inside churches, this one is too striking to resist. And it remains a working cathedral, with prayers given every hour. It's 1 p.m., and I sit for the three-minute ceremony, which is quite calming. After lunch, I explore a bit more of the town before heading to Stonehenge.

Once believed to be a Druid ceremonial site, Stonehenge is now thought to have pre-dated the Druids. It is a small site covered in tourists (up to 8000 visit daily during high season with 32,000 arriving for summer solstice), making photography tricky. Everyone enters through the visitor's center across the street before using a tunnel under the street to access the sight. It is odd that such a notable location is right off a main road, but that's modern planning for you. Due to vandalism and erosion concerns, one can no longer walk up to the stones but rather admire them from afar. I do what I can photographically from my fenced-off vantage point, trying to set it as a backdrop to an impressive sky forming above it. Then it's back to Salisbury for a bit before the train to Waterloo Station.

OFF THE BEATEN PATH IN BATH

The city of Bath was first established as a spa resort with the Latin name *Aquae Sulis* ("the waters of Sulis") by the Romans in 43 CE. The hot springs found here are the only ones naturally occurring in the United Kingdom. It became popular as a spa resort during the Georgian era, which led to a significant expansion that left a plethora of Georgian architecture crafted from Bath stone.

I begin my day trip with a walk along the River Avon. To distinguish it from several other rivers of the same name, it is often also known as the Bristol Avon. The name Avon is a cognate of the Welsh word *afon*, meaning "river," making it the River River. This leads me through town, including a popular, expanding shopping area. Eventually, I come to Bath Abbey, where Edgar was crowned king of England in 973. The abbey is one of the largest examples of Perpendicular Gothic architecture in the southwest of England. Its full name is The Abbey Church of Saint Peter and Saint Paul.

The original Roman baths are now contained in a museum. A temple was constructed on the site between 60-70 CE in the first few decades of Roman Britain. The Roman baths—designed for public bathing—were used until the end of Roman rule in Britain in the 5th century. While there are several baths still to be found, only two contain water, and neither is open to swimmers. The Great Bath can be viewed both from above and at ground level. It is filled with tourists and locals, I'm presuming, portraying Roman citizens. The Sacred Spring is much smaller without a tourist in sight. The museum houses artifacts from the Roman period, including objects thrown into the Sacred Spring, presumably as offerings to the goddess.

MIND THE GAP

I have now been on the road this summer for a total of eleven weeks and today marks my return. After a relaxing morning, H and I have lunch then hop a taxi to Heathrow. There is a long line to check-in (the airline's computers are acting up) before our last coffee together (well, coffee for me, hot chocolate for her—she's still trying to replicate that hot chocolate from the Eurostar). After a final farewell, I make my way through security, and we are back to our separate continents till October, when she will be coming out my way for a few weeks.

As I'm flying out of Heathrow, it's a mile till I reach my gate. Onboard, I discover I have a bulk-head seat, meaning I have some legroom for my eleven-hour flight. The entertainment system is good— I only wish I could say the same for the movies I choose to watch. One of these days, I really need to figure out how to sleep on a plane.

It took me some time to adjust to London. Mostly the public transit, to be honest. I'm used to driving everywhere, so having to base my grocery shopping, for instance, on what I can carry (and what could fit in our apartment's small fridge) was different. On days it was raining, I had to subtract one bag so I could hold an umbrella. The frantic pace of the underground also took me a while to adjust to. One time, H was able to get on the train and I wasn't. Damn my manners. One day, a walking tour ended at an unknown tube station, and I had to call H to figure a way back as the tube map made no sense to me. Those experiences made me determined to master the tube map and train timetables, and I left London with a good understanding of both. On the other hand, bus routes continue to confound me, and I only rode on buses when with H.

Dec. 2010 – *Egypt*

I had wanted to visit Egypt since elementary school when my fifth-grade class made a school presentation. I was in charge of narrating the section on ancient Egypt and quickly became enamored with pyramids and hieroglyphics. Around this time, the King Tut exhibit came to Los Angeles, seeing my mom and me standing in a long line, eager to witness history. Unfortunately, my mom would lose her battle with cancer just a few weeks before I set off on this trip. In fact, as the end was approaching, she made me promise to take this trip as she knew how much I'd wanted to see the country. Also, this would be my only time my now fiancée and I could spend some time together before our wedding in April as she was still living in London.

FROM SNOW TO DESERT

Before heading to Cairo, I am spending some time with H in London. Snow since my arrival has been causing delays at Heathrow, and there is concern about our Christmas day flight. This reminds me of last winter's near misses en route to Tunisia. We just need to make it to Cairo on the 25th and then back to Heathrow in early January. During this time in London, I realize that this native Southern Californian doesn't own any clothes warm enough for a London winter.

We arrive in Cairo an hour late, only we're staying in Giza, not Cairo, so it's another hour to our hotel. The following day is a full one, beginning with the pyramids at Giza. The Great Pyramid is the Pyramid of Khufu (or Cheops in Greek). While this is the largest of the pyramids here, I spend most of my time exploring the Pyramid of Khafre. This pyramid is distinct as its top still has some of the limestone casing that once covered the entire pyramid.

While on my way to explore the Great Pyramid, I am pulled beside a camel and a cloth is tied around my head. "Good photo," I'm told. Next thing I know, I'm atop the camel and am being paraded around for more "good photos." Just when I think I'm finally being let down, the owner starts asking for money and it becomes clear that I'm not getting down until he is paid what he feels he is owed. I try to explain that I don't have any money, which he doesn't buy. Thankfully H then appears, gives him some money, and I'm freed.

Still recovering from my camel-jacking, we move on to explore the third pyramid, the Pyramid of Menkaure, the smallest of the three. Just beyond features excellent views of all three pyramids together.

TOUCH, DON'T TOUCH

In all of his talk of Egypt and its pyramids, there is no mention of the Great Sphinx in Herodotus' account. There is most likely because it was buried in sand at the time. When not buried, it is the largest monolith statue in the world. It is also the oldest known monumental sculpture in Egypt and one of the most recognizable statues in the world. Unlike Greek sphinxes that feature the haunches of a lion, the wings of a great bird, and the face and breasts of a woman, the Egyptian sphinx is wingless and male. And, while the Greek sphinx was seen as treacherous and merciless, the Egyptian one was thought of as a guardian, often flanking the entrances to temples.

We're then on to the Egyptian Museum in Cairo, the oldest archaeological museum in the Middle East, housing the most extensive collection of Pharaonic antiquities in the world. It contains over 120,000 items, with a representative amount on display and the remainder in storerooms. Built-in 1901 by an Italian construction company and designed by a French architect, the structure is one of the largest museums in the region. While photos are not allowed, it appears you can touch the exhibits. Oh wait, there's the sign to not touch. Sorry, I noticed it a bit late.

On our way to dinner in Giza, we're paired with another tour group as their bus has decided to stop operating. We make room for them in our bus and head off. While stuck in Cairo's congested traffic, our bus starts acting up too. It's a slow crawl as we can hear the driver grinding gears. There is also a distinct burnt smell in the air surrounding our bus. Somehow, we make it to the restaurant for dinner, a trail of smoke behind us. Before our return to our hotel for the night, the bus is replaced.

STAIRWAY TO HEAVEN

The Pyramid of Djoser is located in the Saqqara necropolis, northwest of the city of Memphis. It was built for the burial of Pharaoh Djoser by his vizier Imhotep during the 27th century BCE. It is the central feature of a vast mortuary complex in an enormous courtyard surrounded by ceremonial structures and decoration. This first Egyptian pyramid consisted of six mastabas (of decreasing size) built atop one another to provide the deceased with steps up to the afterlife. The pyramid originally stood 203 feet (62 meters) tall and was clad in polished white limestone. This step pyramid is considered to be the earliest large-scale cut stone construction made by man.

Next, it's back to Cairo for a visit to the Saladin Citadel. The location, part of the Muqattam Hills near the center of Cairo, was once famous for its fresh breeze and grand views of the city and was fortified by the Ayyubid ruler Salah al-Din (Saladin) between 1176 and 1183 CE, to protect it from the Crusaders. At the time of its construction, it was among the most ambitious military fortification projects of its time. It is now a preserved historical site containing mosques and museums.

Lastly, it's a stop in Islamic Cairo, where I snap a few photos before the day's light fades. The name "Islamic" Cairo does not refer to a greater prominence of Muslims in the area but rather to the city's rich history and heritage since its foundation in the early period of Islam. It also distinguishes it from nearby Ancient Egyptian sites of Giza and Memphis. It's been a full day with a thankfully reliable bus.

TWO EVENTFUL NIGHTS

Last night H and I were awoken at 3 a.m. by persistent pounding at our hotel room's door. I groggily arise and make my way in the dark to the door. The peephole reveals two men, one local and one Western-looking. Upon opening the door, I'm asked by the Westerner, "Are you Mac?" "No," I reply. "Damn, have the wrong room," he mumbles as they both leave, and I go back to bed.

Tonight, it's an overnight train from Cairo to Luxor. Due to Cairo's ungodly traffic, we barely make it to the station on time. Our room is next to the porter's, so we're served dinner first. We decide to take advantage of this and head to the restroom while everyone else is still eating dinner—a brilliant idea, except that the electricity goes out halfway through my visit. Between trying to figure out how to flush the toilet and operate the sink, I slam my thumb in the bathroom door. I manage to find my way back to our room and fumble around in the dark, getting ready for bed and finding a bandage.

The night's ride is filled with jerks and bumps, and I don't get much sleep. It also doesn't help that I'm a little too long for the bed, so I have to try to sleep with my knees bent. In the morning, we head to the boat that will be our home for the next three nights to drop off our bags. I want nothing more than to crawl into bed, but we have a temple to explore. I soon notice that our local guide that ends every statement with "why?". At first, I thought he was soliciting answers but soon realized that it was his way to set up his response. It reminds me of a college professor I once had who would pause mid-sentence while lecturing. Again, I initially assumed he was giving us time to catch up with his thinking, but I now believe it was just to gather his thoughts.

KARNAK THE MAGNIFICENT

Few things can keep me awake and alert after only a few hours' sleep. One of them is impressive ruins, and that's what's to be found at the Karnak Temple Complex. We get there by taking a carriage ride from our boat, where our luggage will await our return. There's nothing like a horse-drawn carriage amidst Egyptian traffic to get the juices flowing in the morning.

Karnak comprises a vast mix of ruined temples, chapels, pylons, and other buildings and was constructed over a thirteen-hundred-year period. Specifically, construction at the complex began during the reign of Senusret I in the Middle Kingdom (around 2000–1700 BCE) and continued into the Ptolemaic Kingdom (305–30 BCE). The history of the Karnak complex is largely the history of Thebes (now Luxor) and its changing role in the culture. It is the largest temple complex ever built by man and represents the combined achievement of many generations of ancient builders.

The central region of the site, which takes up the most significant amount of space, is dedicated to Amun-Ra, a male god associated with Thebes. The area immediately around his main sanctuary was known in antiquity as Ipet-Sun, or "the most select of places." To the south of the central location is a smaller region dedicated to his wife, the goddess Mut. Karnak would have made a great impression on ancient visitors. As our guide tells us, the numerous pillars and vast enclosure walls were painted white with the reliefs and inscriptions picked out in brilliant jewel-like colors. It is by far the most impressive Egyptian ruins we've encountered so far.

SLOW BOAT TO EDFU

In the morning, we are supposed to stop by Edfu Temple, but we are running behind schedule. Rumor has it that only one of our boat's three engines is working, and we are progressing at a crawl. So, H and I spend the morning on the upper deck, getting some sun, drinking mocktails, and playing cards.

The Temple of Edfu is located on the west bank of the Nile River between Esna and Aswan. It is the second-largest temple in Egypt after Karnak. The temple, dedicated to the falcon god Horus, was built in the Ptolemaic period between 237 and 57 BCE. The temple was buried under centuries of sand and silt until the 19th century when a French Egyptologist rediscovered the site. The complex is one of the most well-preserved sites found in Egypt today. Its architecture is very much intact, and the building contains an abundance of legible inscriptions on its walls.

Several of the inscriptions found at the temple describe the conflict between Horus, the deity of the fertile lands near the Nile, and Seth, the god of the surrounding Egyptian desert, as Horus seeks revenge for the murder of his father, Osiris. This story would have been ceremoniously recreated by the ancient Egyptians each year at the temple complex.

By the time we arrive in the late afternoon, the sun is waning, and rain is in the air. Before the rain starts, I snap a few photos before heading inside for shelter. In early Christian times, persecuted Christians used to use these temples for shelter, though they would also desecrate the faces of the pagan gods. After the rain, the lighting is terrific, so it's time for more exploration and photos.

JIGSAW TEMPLE

Yesterday's six-hour delay has now become a twelve-hour delay, so more sunbathing, mocktails, and cards. And a few random photos of the shoreline. Even the staff seem to be getting bored, as a return to our room before lunch finds an alligator made from towels, the non-operational TV's remote control, and one of my hats. We finally arrive in Aswan in the mid-afternoon and disembark for some sightseeing.

First up: Aswan's High Dam. Constructed in the 1960s, the High Dam was added to the Low Dam, completed in 1902. Before the dams were built, the River Nile flooded each year during late summer, as water flowed down the valley from its East African basin. The winds on top of the dam are high, making photo taking challenging. The High Dam also formed Lake Nasser, the world's largest artificial lake, running through Egypt and into Sudan.

Again, the light is fading, and we still have a temple to visit: Philae Temple, which was dismantled and reassembled on Agilika Island, about 550 meters from its original home on Philae Island. The temple, dedicated to the goddess Isis, is now in a setting that has been landscaped to match its original location. We're able to catch one of the last boats of the day. While not as extensive or impressive as Karnak, it is incredible to think that forty years ago, this site was underwater after the completion of the High Dam. In an engineering feat to rival the ancients, the original island was surrounded by a dam, and the inside pumped dry. Then every stone block of the temple complex was labeled and removed, later to be assembled, like a giant jigsaw puzzle, on the higher ground of Agilika Island. The whole project took ten years. We're only given an hour to explore the site.

ABU SIMBEL

It's a 2:30 a.m. wake-up call to catch a 4:00 a.m. police-escorted convoy of buses, vans, and cars to Abu Simbel. The convoy is a requirement for all tourists due to security concerns. It seems that virtually all tourists travel to Abu Simbel this way on a day trip. However, flights from Aswan are also available.

The twin temples of Abu Simbel were initially carved out of a mountainside during the reign of Pharaoh Ramesses II in the 13th century BCE, as a lasting monument to himself and his queen Nefertari, to commemorate his victory at the Battle of Kadesh, and to intimidate his Nubian neighbors. However, the complex was relocated in its entirety in 1968, on an artificial hill made from a domed structure, high above the Aswan High Dam reservoir. The relocation of the temples was necessary to avoid their being submerged during the creation of Lake Nasser, the massive artificial water reservoir formed after the building of the Aswan High Dam on the Nile River.

It's a three-hour bus ride to Abu Simbel. As we left at 4 a.m., we're here at 7 a.m., though it takes a good fifteen minutes to get our tickets and to get inside the complex, and then it's a five-minute walk to the complex. I'm keeping this in mind as we depart at 9 a.m. I wander around the Great Temple before I squeeze myself in. Photographing inside tombs is not allowed, so my interest is quickly fading in this rush of people. I work my way back out then explore the Small Temple, which was built to honor both Hathor as the goddess of love/music and Nefertari as a deified queen. I then head to the over-priced café for some coffee, where I nearly start an international incident with a group of large Italian women.

ANOTHER CAMEL

We arrive back in Aswan in time for lunch, then a little downtime till a felucca ride. As we've spent the past three days on a boat (and we'd just spent six hours on a bus to spend two hours at a temple), I'm not thrilled to be on another boat. That said, the ride is pleasant and takes us to an island botanic garden. The garden itself isn't worth the price of admission, but the views from the island it resides on are.

It's yet another boat taking us to a Nubian village for the night. When we come ashore, I'm the first off, only to discover that this stop is solely for those who wanted to ride a camel into the village—nearly everyone else is still on the boat. Oh well, I guess I'm going by camel. I'm okay until I notice that the rest of my group is being led up a hill, whereas I'm being led down. It turns out to be a shakedown for a tip, but I hold out until I'm rejoined with my group and let our guide deal with my handler.

In the morning, we visit the Temple of Kom Ombo, an unusual double temple built during the Ptolemaic dynasty. Some additions to it were later made during the Roman period. The building is unique because its 'double' design meant that there were courts, halls, sanctuaries, and rooms duplicated for two sets of gods. The southern half of the temple was dedicated to the crocodile-headed god Sobek, god of fertility, while the northern temple was dedicated to the falcon-headed god Horus. The temple is atypical as everything is perfectly symmetrical along the central axis. The temple was started by Ptolemy VI (180-145 BCE) at the beginning of his reign and added to by other Ptolemys, most notably Ptolemy XIII (51-47 BCE), who built the inner and outer hypostyle halls.

TEMPLES AND TOMBS

In the early afternoon, we return to Luxor, where we will spend our last two nights in Egypt. After a restful afternoon, we head out to a nearby market, where the high-pressure sales ensue. Stop and you will be negotiating whether you want to or not. We pop into a shop overflowing with bric-a-brac—my kind of shop—and then head to dinner. It's another long day tomorrow, including two more temples.

Deir el-Bahari ("The Northern Monastery") is a complex of mortuary temples and tombs located on the west bank of the Nile, opposite the city of Luxor. The focal point of the Deir el-Bahari complex is the Djeser-Djeseru, the Mortuary Temple of Hatshepsut. It is a colonnaded structure, which was designed and implemented by Senemut, royal steward and architect of Hatshepsut, to serve for her posthumous worship and to honor the glory of Amun. The unusual form of Hatshepsut's temple is explained by the choice of location, in the valley basin of Deir el-Bahari, surrounded by steep cliffs.

With the 2006 discovery of a new chamber and the 2008 discovery of two further tomb entrances, the Valley of Kings is known to contain 63 tombs and chambers (ranging in size from a simple pit to a complex tomb with over 120 sections). For nearly 500 years, from the 16th to 11th century BCE, these rock-cut tombs were excavated for the pharaohs and powerful nobles of the time. Most of the tombs are not open to the public. While here, we visit the tombs of Ramses I, IV, and IX. The tomb of Ramses IV is the largest and most impressive. Photography is not allowed anywhere on the site, though books of photos are available for sale around every corner.

MORE TEMPLES AND TOMBS

Today we have a free day and have decided to head off to two sights on our own. First up is Habu Temple, the name commonly given to the Mortuary Temple of Ramses III, a New Kingdom period structure on the West Bank of Luxor. Aside from its inherent size and architectural and artistic importance, the temple is probably best known as the source of inscribed reliefs depicting the arrival and defeat of the Sea Peoples during the reign of Ramses III. It is an incredible sight. The carvings here are the deepest of any temple we've visited in Egypt, and there remain some areas wonderfully colored. It is well worth a visit.

While visiting, H and I get separated when I encounter who looks like an official. He tells me he can let me into areas tourists aren't typically allowed. I follow him to a few inner chambers before he offers to take my photo and then asks for money while blocking the exit. As we're heading out the next day, I do not have much local currency left, and he seems offended when I offer him what I have. Thankfully, I hear H calling for me and am able to escape.

Our last stop in Egypt is Deir el-Medina, an ancient Egyptian village that was home to the artisans who worked on the tombs in the Valley of the Kings during the 18th to 20th dynasties of the New Kingdom period (around 1550–1080 BCE). While these workers were well paid, they were not allowed to leave the area in order to keep the location of the royal tombs a secret. As such, they spent their free time working on their own tombs. Photos are not allowed in the tombs and cameras are confiscated at the door. Even though leaving my camera was involuntary, a tip is suggested when retrieving it —there's a shock.

OUT OF AFRICA

It's a 5:00 a.m. rise so that we can get to Luxor airport three hours before our flight to Cairo. On our return to Luxor last night, there was some disturbance outside a Coptic Christian church. I think it's a good thing we are flying out today. The conveyor belt carrying our flight's baggage is broken, and checked bags are piled here, there, and everywhere behind the check-in counter. I am sure we will never see our bags again.

Once in Cairo, we have a seven-hour layover. One problem: One has to go through security before reaching the ticket counters, which don't open for four hours, and they are located in a no-man's-land. There's nothing to eat or drink till you get through Customs, but you can't get through Customs without a boarding pass, which you can only get at the ticket counter. It takes 30 minutes of pleading with seven people before we are let out of this area and allowed to get some food. I leave this to H as she has a far better smile. After a leisurely lunch, we're back through security to a still unopened ticket counter.

Security is everywhere in Egypt, along with metal detectors and x-ray machines. Want to enter a hotel? You pass through an x-ray machine with a guard sitting beside it. Want to enter most sites? Same thing. In 1997, Islamist militants massacred 58 tourists and 4 Egyptians at Deir el-Bahri, so it's understandable. However, I'm not convinced that all of the metal detectors and x-ray machines actually work. Egyptian officials also seem to love admission tickets. In all, I have accumulated 15, averaging 50 Egyptian pounds each (around $8.50). Considering the hundreds if not thousands of tourists at each site, it's not a bad racket.

IN MEMORIUM

The first time I tried out my present camera was at a botanical garden on my mom's birthday, a year after she was diagnosed with cancer. After retiring, she had become an avid gardener, and this seemed an ideal spot to spend the day. Unfortunately, she lost her six-year battle with cancer a few weeks before I left on this trip. Knowing my love of travel, she made me promise to go on this trip even though some thought I shouldn't. She knew how much I'd always wanted to see Egypt and that I'd be spending the trip with my fiancée.

It was through my mom that I developed the travel bug. Her travels included the U.K., Mexico, Canada, and sailing on the RMS Queen Mary. Later in life, she traveled with my grandmother—they'd often schedule an annual cruise when not flying back to England to visit relatives. After my grandmother passed, she was even able to persuade my father to get a passport—not bad for a man who doesn't like flying. She always encouraged my travels and never questioned my sometimes off-the-beaten-path destinations.

I had hoped that this trip would be an escape, but I was only reminded that she would not be there when I got home to tell my stories to. And she'd never see any more of my photos. She was a kind spirit that showed incredible strength and bravery during her battle with cancer. She loved spending time with friends and family and always put others' needs above her own. Yet, she was also strong-willed and independent. I could always leave it to my mom to tell it to me straight while still being encouraging. The world is a lesser place without her.

ALSO BY JEREMIAH A. GILBERT

POETRY

In a Strange Land

Pagan Blues

The Pursuing Silence

One Hand Clapping: Zen Mountain Poems

TRAVEL

Can't Get Here from There: Fifty Tales of Travel

www.ingramcontent.com/pod-product-compliance
Lightning Source LLC
LaVergne TN
LVHW092356170726
843489LV00001B/215